Euripides: Medea

DUCKWORTH COMPANIONS
TO GREEK AND ROMAN TRAGEDY

Euripides: Medea

William Allan

Duckworth

This impression 2008
First published in 2002 by
Gerald Duckworth & Co. Ltd.
90-93 Cowcross Street, London EC1M 6BF
Tel: 020 7490 7300
Fax: 020 7490 0080
inquiries@duckworth-publishers.co.uk
www.ducknet.co.uk

A catalogue record for this book is available
from the British Library

ISBN 978 0 7156 3187 4

Typeset by Ray Davies
Printed and bound in Great Britain by
CPI Antony Rowe, Eastbourne

Contents

For my teachers at
Glenrothes High School

Preface

Greek tragedy remains a powerful, enjoyable, and relevant creative medium, and perhaps no work of classical Greek drama enjoys more popularity and influence today than Euripides' *Medea*. This book aims to set the play in its mythical, theatrical, and social context, and to explore in detail the work's dramatic technique and central ideas. The chapters try to do justice both to the drama's visceral emotional force and to its capacity to stimulate debate about a variety of social, political, and ethical problems which are as much a part of our world as that of the ancient Greeks.

My thanks go to Tom Harrison, Series Editor, and Deborah Blake, Editorial Director at Duckworth, for their generous advice and assistance. I was fortunate to have the opportunity of discussing *Medea* with the late Charles Segal; his interest, insights, and encouragement were of the greatest value to me. I dedicate the book to my high school teachers: Dennis Duncan, David Neilson, David Potter, and the late Charles Wallace. They first sparked my interest in literature and encouraged me to study it further. My debt to them is very great.

July 2002   W.R.A.

1

Festival, Myth, and Play

Euripides' *Medea* was first performed in Athens at the City Dionysia of 431 BC. As with any other work of literature, our understanding of the play is greatly enhanced by a sense of its historical context, and so we shall begin our discussion by outlining the social and cultural background to fifth-century Athenian tragedy. The chapter will also sketch *Medea*'s place within Euripides' dramatic career, consider the development of the Medea myth before Euripides, and finally analyse the structure and stagecraft of the play itself.

The particular civic and festival context of Athenian drama illustrates the deep links that existed between the theatre and the wider cultural, political, and religious life of the *polis* (or 'city-state'). For like most surviving Greek tragedies, *Medea* was first performed at the Great or City Dionysia, an urban religious festival held every spring to honour Dionysus, the god of theatre.[1] The City Dionysia was not the only Athenian festival involving poetry, music, and dance, but it was by far the largest and most prestigious dramatic festival, attracting visitors from many Greek cities. The festival began with a large procession through the city to the sanctuary of Dionysus on the southern side of the Acropolis, followed by massive public sacrifices and feasting. Besides the dramatic competitions, there were also junior and senior contests for dithyramb (a choral song in honour of Dionysus), featuring choruses of fifty boys and fifty men from each of the ten tribes of Athens. While each of the five comic dramatists presented only one play, the three tragedians were each allocated an entire day in which to present three tragedies and a satyr play (a kind of mythological burlesque featuring a Chorus of satyrs, beastlike men with a horse's tail and a large, erect phallus). In 431 BC Euripides competed with *Medea*, *Philoctetes*, *Dictys*, and the satyr play *Theristai* ('Reapers'). He won the third (and last) prize (see below).

Though it was certainly a joyous festival, there was more to the City Dionysia than entertainment and revelry. In the course of the fifth century BC Athens used her naval supremacy to build up a large empire of 'allied' states (known in modern scholarship as the Delian League), and at the time of the Dionysia (roughly late March, when the seas could once again be sailed) these subjects had to transport their tribute to Athens, where it was publicly exhibited in the theatre, a strong visual and material token of Athens' imperial power and hegemony. In addition, two pre-performance ceremonies emphasised the city's generosity and loyalty: state benefactors were saluted and honoured for their services, while the mature sons of the Athenian war dead, who had been raised at the state's expense, were awarded suits of armour, paraded before the theatre audience, and granted prestigious front-row seats.[2] Such ceremonies were no doubt intended to confirm Athens' image as a benevolent leader. Moreover, as the high point in the city's dramatic calendar, the Dionysia was also an opportunity for Athens to impress foreign visitors with its cultural (as well as its military) achievements.

The theatre of Dionysus in Athens could accommodate between 15,000 and 20,000 spectators. While the majority were certainly Athenian men, the very presence of women has been doubted by some scholars. The evidence itself is controversial,[3] but when taken together with the religious context of the performance, it suggests that women probably were present, along with other peripheral (i.e. non-citizen) groups such as children, slaves, and foreigners, though not perhaps in large numbers or occupying the best seats.[4] The presence of female spectators will have been of particular significance to the live communal experience of the plays, so many of which explore areas of conflict between the sexes (cf. Chapter 2), but similar considerations also apply to the attendance of slaves, resident aliens, and foreigners (Chapter 3). Although many recent studies of Athenian tragedy claim that it 'defines the male citizen self, and both produces and reproduces the ideology of the civic community',[5] the heterogeneous nature of the audience, as well as the multifarious characters and content of the plays themselves, suggest that tragedy was far more complex in both its appeal and its experience. Rather than simply endorsing Athenian civic ideology, the plays expose the most fundamental tensions and conflicts within Athenian society, and explore its underbelly from a variety of angles. In doing so they are far from promoting the 'reproduction' of an official civic dogma or from being straightforwardly didactic in any sense.

The stage resources of Athenian drama were developed to suit the needs of a large-scale outdoor theatre. The performance area consisted of a large dancing-floor (*orchêstra*) whose exact shape in the fifth century BC remains a matter of dispute. Some think it was round (as it certainly was after the rebuilding work begun by Lycurgus in the late fourth century BC), while others favour a rectangular or trapezoidal area (as in other early theatres).[6] In fact, certainty on most questions relating to the theatre of Dionysus is impossible as there are 'many different ways to combine and interpret [the] remains, which moreover have been variously dated'.[7] Fortunately, however, the precise shape of the *orchêstra* does not significantly affect the dynamics of the action; the important point is that, unlike the modern proscenium-arch theatre, the *orchêstra* offered a performance space flanked by spectators on three sides and a playing area large enough to contain both chorus and actors.

Behind the *orchêstra* stood a single-storey stage-building

(*skênê*), a temporary wooden structure that was put up for the period of the dramatic competitions. The *skênê* was used to represent whatever backdrop the play required (palace, temple, tent, etc.). In *Medea* it represents the house of Jason and Medea in Corinth, a house that Jason has abandoned in favour of the royal palace. Perhaps the most controversial question relating to the theatre of Dionysus is whether in the Classical period there was a raised stage for the actors between the *skênê* and the *orchêstra*.[8] If it did exist, it will have been no more than a low platform in front of the *skênê*, connected by steps to the *orchêstra*. The important point is that there was free movement between the two areas: the tragic chorus occasionally enters, or thinks of entering (cf. *Medea* 1275), the stage-building, and the actors were free to join the chorus in the *orchêstra*. In any case, it is conventional to use the word 'stage' to refer to the playing area as a whole (and this convention will be followed here). If he wished, the dramatist could bring an interior tableau onto the stage by using the *ekkyklêma*, a wheeled platform that could be rolled out from the central double doors of the *skênê*. This is generally used to reveal a scene of carnage within the house (e.g. Sophocles, *Electra* 1458-65, Euripides, *Heracles* 1028-38). Finally, a crane (*mêchanê*) was positioned behind the stage-building and could be used to transport characters (usually gods) through the air and sometimes onto the *skênê* roof or stage. Medea escapes from Corinth in a chariot sent by her grandfather, the sun-god Helios (cf. 1321-2), and this was most probably performed using the crane.

Amidst these basic stage resources the central focus of Greek tragedy is always upon the words and actions of the characters themselves. Every play has a chorus, a group of fifteen men who take on a specific collective identity chosen by the dramatist. Like the *chorêgos* (literally 'chorus leader', the wealthy sponsor who paid for their training),[9] the chorus members had to be Athenian citizens. But their choral identity (male or female,

14

human or divine, free or slave, etc.) is developed in each play to enhance the meaning of the action. Thus it is significant that Medea is made to interact with a chorus of conventional Corinthian women, since this articulates various aspects of her status as both an abandoned wife and a foreigner. Although the actors playing the principal roles were not always Athenian citizens, they were always free-born Greek men; nevertheless, they too adopted a great variety of ethnic, social and gender identities (clearly marked by costume and mask as well as by behaviour and speech). Since speaking parts could be allocated to only three actors (the so-called 'three-actor rule'; there was no limit on the number of silent figures allowed), each actor usually had to play more than one role and it was occasionally necessary to divide the same role between two or even three actors. Before taking on a new role the actor would change his costume and mask behind the *skênê*. The division of parts in *Medea*, as with every other play, is largely a matter of conjecture. One possible division would be Actor 1: Medea; Actor 2: Nurse, Jason; Actor 3: Paidagogos, Creon, Aegeus, Messenger.[10] The two sons of Medea and Jason were played by children; they remain silent while on stage,[11] but are heard crying out in distress from inside the house (1270-8).

Euripides' theatrical career spans the entire second half of the fifth century BC. Born in the 480s, he first competed at the City Dionysia in 455, coming third with a group of plays that included *Peliades* (*The Daughters of Pelias*), a tragedy dramatising an earlier episode in the myth of Medea (see below). Over the next fifty years or so (he died in 407-6) Euripides competed at the Dionysia on 22 occasions (that is, he wrote at least 88 plays, 66 of them tragedies), but he won the first prize only four times in his lifetime (a fifth was awarded posthumously, *c.* 405, for a production including *Bacchae* and *Iphigenia in Aulis*). Yet although Euripides was far less successful in competitive terms than his great predecessor Aeschylus (13 victories) and his rival

Sophocles (18 victories), his work must have been greatly appreciated by the Athenians or he would not have been granted a chorus so many times.

His earliest surviving work, *Alcestis*, took the place of the satyr-play in the production of 438; it combines features of satyric burlesque with tragic themes of suffering and death. Euripides' willingness to combine a variety of tones, a genre-bending style prominent in such later 'happy ending' tragedies as *Ion*, *Helen*, and *Iphigenia in Tauris*, is already in evidence here. From first to last Euripides' plays show a stimulating openness to the intellectual experiments of his time. As a result Aristophanes could in his *Frogs* of 405 parody Euripides as a subversive Sophist, a questioner of ancestral traditions, whether moral, political, social or religious. Yet while it is true that Euripides' work bears the mark of intellectual enquiry most strikingly, whether it be to question the status of women or slaves, or to explore the morality of anthropomorphic gods, it is also true that he *transforms* such issues so as to further the peculiar tragic situation of each play. Moreover, since the surviving plays show such a multiplicity of theme, form, and tone, it is best to get to grips with each individual work itself before relating it to Euripides' theatrical imagination in general and the wider cultural currents of his time.

Medea, performed in 431 BC, is (after *Alcestis*) the second of Euripides' seventeen surviving tragedies. Its companion plays (*Philoctetes*, *Dictys*, *Theristai*) deal with separate myths and survive only in fragments.[12] Considering the massive popularity of both the Medea myth and Euripides' play from antiquity to the present day (see Chapter 5), it may seem surprising that *Medea* won only the third prize. Various explanations have been offered, ranging from the audience's shock at the infanticide to their displeasure with the ambiguous presentation of Aegeus, king of Athens. But the first prize was won by Aeschylus' son Euphorion (perhaps with a production including *Prometheus*

Unbound, which he may have passed off as his father's work) and Sophocles came second, so the competition were hardly complete unknowns. And perhaps (one of) Euripides' other plays that year were not up to scratch; there is no way of knowing, but in any case we should not read too much into *Medea*'s supposed 'failure' in the competition. More significant is the play's production date of 431 BC, only a few months before full-scale war finally broke out between Athens and Sparta. One of Sparta's most powerful allies and a major force in persuading her to attack Athens was Corinth (cf. Thucydides 1.66-71), the setting of *Medea*. The play's contrast between a Corinthian king who expels an innocent woman and an Athenian king who agrees to protect her is no doubt significant. But this detail hardly makes the play an uncomplicated piece of pro-Athenian propaganda (see Chapter 3). And we should steer well clear of the kind of direct relationship between drama and history which led to the biographical fantasy of the Corinthians bribing Euripides to transfer blame for the infanticide from them to Medea.[13]

Before we look in detail at the structure, style, and dramatic technique of the play, it is important that we consider Medea's role in the mythological tradition before Euripides. For this will give us some idea of what a fifth-century audience may have already known about Medea, and so enable us to appreciate more fully Euripides' creative transformation of his inherited material. The figure of Medea belongs to a complex of stories collectively known as the Iolcus cycle,[14] which included Jason's voyage in the ship Argo to Aia in Colchis, Medea's homeland, in search of the Golden Fleece. Aia lay at the distant eastern edge of the world beside the river Ocean. In the earliest surviving reference to the Fleece itself, the seventh-century BC elegiac poet Mimnermus (fr. 11 *IEG*) says, 'Jason would not have brought the great fleece back from Aia, having completed a painful journey and having performed a difficult task for the arrogant Pelias, nor would they [i.e. the Argonauts] have reached the beautiful river Ocean.' Jason was forced to undertake the journey by his uncle Pelias, who had deposed Jason's father Aeson, king of Iolcus, and hoped that Jason would die on such a dangerous quest. Aeëtes, king of Colchis and father of Medea, duly set Jason a series of arduous and seemingly impossible tasks, but Medea fell in love with him and used her magic powers to help Jason secure the Fleece (cf. Pindar, *Pythian* 4.71-251).

The Argo is already described in the *Odyssey* (12.70) as 'known to all', and in Hesiod's *Theogony* (992-1002) Jason is said to have brought Medea back to Iolcus by the will of the gods. The context of the Hesiod passage, a catalogue of goddesses who slept with mortal men, makes it clear that Medea is thought of as immortal and divine. In Pindar, Medea speaks from her 'immortal mouth' (*Pythian* 4.11). By contrast, Euripides presents Medea as a fully mortal woman, but uses her divine descent to stunning effect in the final scene of the play (cf. Chapter 4). As well as her divinity, early poetry also stresses Medea's skill in the use of drugs. As granddaughter of Helios and niece of Circe (Aeëtes' sister), Medea is associated by descent with the power of magic. Moreover, her name suggests *mêdesthai* ('to devise'; cf. 401-2) and her mother is the nymph Iduia ('she who knows'; cf. *Theogony* 956-62).

According to the cyclic epic *Nostoi* (fr. 6 *EGF*), Medea used her magic skills to rejuvenate Jason's father Aeson, while the lyric poet Simonides has her rejuvenate Jason himself (fr. 548 *PMG*; cf. Pherecydes *FGrH* 3 F 113).[15] But the most famous (and disturbing) instance of Medea's magic powers of rejuvenation is her deception of the daughters of Pelias. Medea chopped up an old ram and boiled it in a cauldron, making it young again. Having persuaded the daughters of Pelias to do the same to their father, she then withheld the magic ingredients so that Pelias, Jason's wicked uncle, remained a human stew. This was a popular episode in Archaic art, though the murder itself is never shown; instead the ram is depicted rising from the cauldron, foreshadowing the gruesome contrast with Pelias.[16] In Euripides' play the motif of magically destroying an enemy through his children is adapted so that Creon's daughter, poisoned by Medea's drugs, kills her own father (1204-21). Medea herself mentions the 'most painful' death of Pelias at the hands of his children (486-7; cf. 9-10), but as with her other great crime, the murder of her brother Apsyrtus (cf. 166-7, 1334), these horrific acts are used to stress how much Medea has done for Jason and how much she has sacrificed for him.

The fullest pre-Euripidean account of Medea and Jason's relationship is that found in Pindar's fourth Pythian ode, and it is interesting to compare the two poets' contrasting versions of events in Colchis. Pindar's ode, the longest surviving epinician (or victory song), was written for Arcesilas of Cyrene in North Africa, who won the chariot race at Delphi in 462 BC. Arcesilas' family claimed descent from Euphamus, one of the Argonauts, and this genealogical link is the basis for Pindar's narration of the Argonautic myth. According to Pindar, Aphrodite taught Jason to use love charms to seduce the Colchian princess 'so that he might take away Medea's respect for her parents' (*Pythian* 4.218).[17] Yet despite Medea's status here as the object of Jason's seduction, there is little sense in Pindar that Medea is in any way a victim of Jason's mission. In Euripides, by contrast, her suffering as a result of her 'maddened heart' is stressed emphatically, not only by Medea herself (485), but also by the Nurse (8) and the Chorus (432). Jason even tries to exploit Aphrodite's role to argue that Medea was not responsible for her actions and can therefore take no credit for her good deeds towards him (526-31), but his argument is unconvincing since it is a basic feature of Greek religious thought that external divine influence does not preclude individual mortal responsibility (regardless of whether the actions themselves are good or bad).[18] Significantly, whereas Pindar presents Jason as slaying the snake that guarded the Golden Fleece (4.249), Euripides' Medea says that she killed it herself (480-2): the stress on Medea's heroic courage both magnifies her 'unfeminine' character (cf. Chapter 2) and diminishes the stature of Jason. In short, whereas Pindar depicts the power of Medea and Jason's erotic attraction and their 'sweet marriage and mutual agreement' (*Pythian* 4.222-3), Euripides explores the bitter aftermath of that relationship's betrayal.

Apart from epic and lyric poetry, Medea also appeared in a number of tragedies before 431 BC. Indeed *Peliades* (*The Daughters of Pelias*), part of Euripides' first production in 455, shows an early creative engagement with the Medea myth.[19] As the title suggests, the play dramatised Medea's deception of the daughters of Pelias and the murder of their father.[20] Significantly, as in her later name play, Medea uses a man's lack of male offspring to ensure that her enemies are punished. For in *Medea* she exploits Aegeus' infertility to secure a place of refuge at Athens (716-22) before inflicting childlessness upon Jason, while in *Peliades* she offers to help amend the aged Pelias' lack of sons by making him young and virile again. The fragmentary ancient hypothesis (or summary) of *Peliades* reports that at the end of the play Medea signalled her success to Jason from the roof of the palace. By contrast, when she appears in the final scene of *Medea* above the roof of her house, it is to announce to Jason that his punishment has been perfected.

It used to be thought that Sophocles treated the Pelias episode in his *Rhizotomoi* (or *Root-Cutters*: *TrGF* IV 534-6),[21] but this is far from certain, for it may have presented an earlier episode in Colchis, where Medea used the root of the plant Prometheion to protect Jason in the tasks set him by Aeëtes. In any case, even if Sophocles' play was set in Iolcus, we have no way of dating it relative to Euripides' *Peliades*. While neither Aeschylus nor Euripides seem to have written a play based on events in Colchis, Sophocles' *Colchides* (*The Women of Colchis*: *TrGF* IV 337-49) told how Jason performed the tasks and escaped from Colchis with Medea's help. The play is particularly notable for the fact that Medea is made to kill her young brother Apsyrtus in the palace of Aeëtes.[22] By contrast, in our earliest source for the killing (Pherecydes *FGrH* 3 F 32), Medea takes her brother from the house and kills him during the Colchian's pursuit of the Argo, cutting his body into pieces and scattering them in the sea so that Aeëtes is forced to stop and collect them for burial. In *Medea*, however, Euripides follows the Sophoclean version and has Apsyrtus killed at the family hearth (1334), an act of kin murder within the *oikos* which prefigures Medea's infanticide.

After killing her children in Corinth, Medea flees to Athens and lives with king Aegeus (cf. 1384-5). Although her stay there falls outside the dramatic frame of *Medea*, it underlies the *Aegeus* plays of both Sophocles and Euripides. The meagre fragments of Sophocles' *Aegeus* (*TrGF* IV 19-25) make it very hard to reconstruct the plot, but Euripides' version can be pieced together more fully.[23] When Theseus arrived in Athens, Medea recognised his true identity as Aegeus' son. But since she feared that Theseus might be a threat to her position, she persuaded Aegeus to send him against the bull of Marathon. Upon Theseus' triumphant return Medea tried to poison him but Aegeus recognised his son at the last moment and Medea was banished from Athens.[24] Though we cannot be sure of the date of either Sophocles' or Euripides' *Aegeus*, it has been rightly pointed out that 'the connexion between Aegeus and Medea was long established and the audience did not need to have seen the *Aegeus* to understand the Aegeus scene in the *Medea*'.[25] Moreover, Medea's dangerous future in Athens will have influenced how an Athenian audience reacted not only to the Aegeus scene, but to the play as a whole, and it is all the more remarkable that, despite Medea's threat to Athens,

21

Euripides presents her (so the following chapters argue) as a largely sympathetic figure.

No less striking is the fact that while other tragedies present Medea's experiences in Colchis, Iolcus, and Athens, only *Medea* deals with events in Corinth. Medea herself was an important figure in Corinthian tradition, but a comparison of these accounts with Euripides' handling of the myth reveals the fundamental originality of his conception. Around 700 BC the Corinthian poet Eumelus composed his epic *Corinthiaca* in which Medea is summoned by the Corinthians from Iolcus and made queen (her father Aeëtes had ruled in Corinth before becoming king of Colchis).[26] Hera promises Medea that she will make her children immortal, but when Medea leaves them in Hera's sanctuary, they perish. Jason and Medea separate and leave Corinth, but their children are honoured by the Corinthians with a cult. So here we have a pre-Euripidean version in which Medea kills her children *accidentally*.

Moreover, the scholia to line 264 of *Medea* speak of two other traditions which ascribe responsibility for the deaths not to Medea, but to others. The second-century BC grammarian Parmeniscus records a version in which the Corinthians resent being ruled by the foreigner Medea and so kill her children (seven sons and seven daughters), who have taken sanctuary in the temple of Hera. In another version, attributed to Creophylus,[27] Creon's relatives kill the children to avenge Medea's murder of Creon and then spread a rumour that Medea killed the children herself. Though we cannot be certain to what extent these accounts contain details that pre-date Euripides, several passages in *Medea* suggest that Euripides knew of a traditional version in which the children were killed by Creon's family (cf. 1060-1, 1238-9, 1303-5). Thus, there are two different accounts of the children's death in pre-Euripidean myth: (1) Medea kills her children unintentionally; and (2) others kill the children intentionally. In other words, Euripides is the first recorded source to present Medea *deliberately killing her own children*. Though it has recently been doubted whether Euripides himself invented this version of events, it still seems a plausible explanation.[28] Similarly, Euripides is the first to present Jason abandoning Medea for another woman, and one may see the poet giving Medea a novel motive (avenging Jason's betrayal) for her new crimes (the poisoning of Jason's young bride and the murder of her own children).

However, according to a hypothesis to *Medea*, some sources claimed that Euripides adapted his play from a *Medea* by Neophron, a tragic poet said to have written 120 plays, though *Medea* is the only title to survive. The three fragments of Neophron's play (*TrGF* I 92-4) do indeed show some marked connections to Euripides: Aegeus comes to ask for Medea's help in deciphering the Delphic oracle's response (cf. 663-88); Medea debates with herself whether to kill her children (cf. 1042-80); Medea predicts Jason's death by hanging (cf. 1386-8). While it has been argued on stylistic grounds that Neophron was probably a fourth-century BC dramatist who in fact adapted Euripides' work,[29] Neophron's priority has been defended by a number of scholars.[30] Yet many of the arguments on either side seem rather subjective,[31] and given the paucity of our sources, we cannot be entirely certain who came first or who invented what, even if on balance the priority of Euripides' version seems (to me at any rate) more compelling.[32] In any case, it is important that such questions of innovation and priority do not distract us from appreciating the uniqueness and particularity of Euripides' work.[33] Euripides has constructed his plot so that Medea's revenge, and her infanticide in particular, have an overwhelmingly powerful impact. From the inherited material Euripides has created something uniquely shocking and tragic.

In order to appreciate how such effects are achieved we have to look closely at the shape and movement of the play. The structure of every Greek tragedy is articulated at the most fundamental level by the alternation between actors' spoken dialogue and choral song, a pattern that is flexible rather than fixed and different from play to play. As it happens, *Medea* has the so-called 'classical' (but in reality untypical) structure of opening scene (*prologos*), choral entry song (*parodos*), five scenes (*epeisodia*), each followed by a choral song (*stasimon*), and exit-scene (*exodos*). But such a cursory formal analysis reveals nothing about the particular dynamics of the play. For this we must look in much greater detail at the stragecraft of each individual scene and song, and this is what the rest of the chapter aims to do.[34] Although the play is discussed (for the sake of structural clarity) as a sequence of differentiated formal elements, we shall see that the individual scenes and songs are part of a larger, cohesive, and dramatically significant structure, which is the experience and impact of the play as a whole.

Opening scene (*prologos*) 1-130

The prologue consists of three distinct but interconnected parts:[35] a formal opening speech by the Nurse (1-48),[36] a dialogue-scene between the Nurse and the Paidagogos (49-95), and a lyric exchange (sung and chanted anapaests) between Medea and the Nurse (96-130). The Nurse's opening remarks on the mythical background to the play (the Argo's voyage, the death of Pelias, Jason and Medea's exile to Corinth) are remarkable for being an extended wish that the legendary past be undone: 'If only the Argo had never sailed ...' (1-15). Significantly, the Nurse's monologue introduces us to the dramatic situation from a perspective that is sympathetic to Medea. Jason, she says, has 'betrayed' (17) his wife and sons by marrying Creon's daughter. Medea, now abandoned, bewails Jason's broken oaths and false promises (21-3), an expression of Jason's treachery that will recur throughout the play (e.g. 160-5, 168-70, 208-13, 439-41, 492-8, 1392). Though Medea does not appear in the opening scene, the Nurse vividly pictures her off-stage condition inside the house, where she lies weeping and refusing to eat or see friends (24-33). The house is thus made a symbol of Medea's desolation and sense of betrayal.

The Nurse's speech is programmatic for the entire plot-structure in another important respect, for she raises the fearful possibility of Medea harming her own children: 'She hates her children and does not delight to see them. I fear her in case she is planning something unexpected' (36-7). The entry of the Paidagogos (literally 'child-leader') with Medea and Jason's two sons (46ff.) sharpens the foreboding of maternal violence by showing us its potential victims. The focus on innocent childhood is intensified by the identity of the two speakers, Medea's childhood Nurse and the tutor of Medea's own children. Moreover, this is the only scene in extant tragedy between two slaves,[37] and their view of the domestic crisis 'from below' generates a particular sympathy for Medea and her children. The familiarity of their conversation contrasts with the Nurse's formal monologue, creating a more intimate domestic atmosphere. The reluctant Paidagogos is forced to reveal that Creon has another blow in store for Medea: she and her children are to be exiled from Corinth (61-73). Both slaves find Creon's decision cruel and excessive, and when the Nurse wonders that Jason can allow his children to be banished, the Paidagogos sums up their father's new loyalties: 'Old family ties have been left behind for new ones; that man is no friend to our house' (76-7). By urging the Nurse not to tell Medea the bad news (80-1), the Paidagogos creates even more sympathy for her, since from Medea's first entry (214ff.) the audience know that there is more distress in store for her. The Nurse breaks off the dialogue by sending the children back into the house, but she instructs the Paidagogos to keep them well away from Medea (89-91).

The children's movement towards the house is accompanied

by Medea's first cries of despair from inside it (96-7). The effect is ominous, as Medea's sons enter a house of lamentation.[38] The spoken iambics of the slaves' dialogue give way to Medea's agitated lyric anapaests (96-7, 111-14) and the Nurse's less frantic, but still emotionally heightened, recitative (or chanted) anapaests (98-110, 115-30).[39] While Medea wishes she were dead (97), the Nurse hurries the children into the house and warns them not to approach their mother, whose spirit she describes as 'swollen [in anger], hard to resist' (109). The adjectives well express Medea's formidable temper. As the children exit, Medea wishes they too would die with their father: 'may the whole house be destroyed!', she screams from within (114). Dreading that innocent children might be punished for the sins of their father, the Nurse now criticises Medea from her low social position, relating her mistress's savage temper to her insulted royal status (119-21).

First choral song (*parodos*) 131-213

In response to Medea's cries the Chorus of fifteen Corinthian women enter from the city.[40] The prologue's gradual movement from individual speech to shared song and recitative makes for a skilful transition to the Chorus' entrance song. At first they sing and dance in the anapaestic metre used by Medea and the Nurse, but quickly move into dactylic / iambic (131-8), and then more elaborate polymetric forms (148-58, 173-83), as they develop their own distinctive voice within the action. The Chorus are sympathetic to Medea and anxious for the welfare of her household: it is immediately clear that their female choral identity will have an important influence on their response to Medea's crisis. The Nurse replies, 'There is no household; it's gone' (139), but her measured explanation is followed by Medea's impassioned cry from inside the house, wishing that she were dead (144-7).

The Chorus now sing the first of two metrically identical songs, the first (*strophê*) directed towards Medea (148-58), the second (*antistrophê*) towards the Nurse (173-83). In the strophe they criticise Medea's desire for death, calling her a 'foolish woman' (152), but they also reassure her that Zeus will defend her cause. In her reply Medea takes up the Chorus' invocation of Zeus, Earth, and light, the gods of oath-taking (148, 157), and calls upon Themis and Artemis to witness Jason's betrayal of his pledge (159-61). She wishes once more for vengeance upon Jason. Significantly, however, she also envisages the destruction of Jason's new bride and the royal palace (162-5). Medea's off-stage cries thus raise multiple targets for her anger: herself, her children, Jason, Creon's daughter, and the royal household. As one scholar has noted, Euripides has skilfully 'conceived the idea of twofold dramatic misdirection in the prologue (the fear of suicide, the possibility that Medea may kill Jason), so ingeniously and economically combined with true forecasts (danger to the children, killing of *tyrannoi* ["rulers"]) ... *all four* of these threats feature in Medea's first utterances (heard from within): 96-7, 111-14, 144-7, 160-7'.[41] By having Medea pray for a revenge that has not yet taken firm shape, suspense is created over the identity of her final victims. As the Nurse goes in to speak with her mistress, the Chorus recall Medea's curses upon Jason and her invocations of divine support (205-13).

Second scene (first *epeisodion*) 214-409

Medea enters from the house, followed by the Nurse. She begins by addressing the Chorus of Corinthian women, and the significant contrast between her previous off-stage exclamations and her self-possessed speech ensures that 'we understand the effort that her apparent calm is costing her'.[42] Since her abandonment by Jason has left Medea friendless and vulnerable, her long opening speech is geared to win the Chorus' sympathy and

support. Medea outlines her pitiful situation point by point:
Jason's treachery (225-9), her powerlessness as a woman (230-51), and her desperate status as a foreigner without relatives to
protect her (255-8). The scale and detail of the second argument
are particularly striking (cf. Chapter 2), as Medea emphasises
the disadvantages of being female and appeals to the Chorus'
shared sense of sexual misfortune. The purpose of Medea's
speech becomes clear in its closing lines, when she asks the
Chorus to keep silent about her (still developing) plan to punish
Jason (259-63). They promptly agree to Jason's 'just' punishment and express sympathy for Medea's predicament (267-8).
But just as Medea secures their support, the Chorus announce
Creon's arrival (269-70), and since we, unlike the Chorus, have
already heard of Creon's decision to banish Medea and her
children (cf. 69-72), his entry 'to announce his new plans' (270)
forbodes a further unexpected blow to her fortunes.

Creon does not delay his bad news. His opening words are
blunt and aggressive ('You there, with your scowling face ...',
271) and he orders Medea to leave Corinth immediately, taking
both her children. While it is true that from here on 'the play
resolves itself into a formally austere sequence of two-actor
confrontations, punctuated by Medea's monologues and articulated by choral song',[43] there is no sense of monotony in the
sequence since each confrontation brings about a new development in the plot and shows the details of Medea's plan from a
new perspective. Medea's confrontation with Creon drastically
limits the time available to perfect her revenge, as she is first
banished directly (272-6), and then granted one day to prepare
her departure (350-6). The increased pressure propels the action forward and tests Medea's ingenuity. Having failed to
convince Creon that her reputation for cleverness is undeserved
(292-305), she resorts to the most powerful means of entreaty
possible, clasping Creon's knees in ritual supplication (324ff.).
But Creon remains unmoved (he loves his own house, he says,

more than he respects Medea's suppliant prayers: 326-7) and it is only when Medea modifies her plea to ask for just one day's respite that Creon reluctantly agrees. Ironically, in view of her future actions (against his and her own children), Medea persuades Creon by appealing to his love as a parent (344-5).

Although Creon returns to his palace insisting that Medea and her children must either leave Corinth or die (351-4), we see that he has in fact failed to impose his original decision.[44] This is a crucial turning point in the action, for it gives Medea a brief but priceless opportunity to perfect her revenge, as her following speech makes clear. Not only does she answer the pessimistic Chorus (cf. 357-63) in a tone of unexpected confidence and defiance, but she also puts the previous confrontation in a new light by describing her supplication of Creon as tactical 'fawning' (368-9) and by deriding Creon's 'foolishness' (371). Continuing the play's use of plot misdirection, Medea now says she will kill Creon, his daughter, and *Jason* as well (374-5; cf. 287-9, 366-7), a prediction which colours the following scene, where Jason enters to justify his conduct to Medea (446ff.). Finally, as preparation for the arrival of a rescuer (cf. 663ff.), Medea wonders if she will find a safe refuge from her crimes (386-91; cf. 359-60). If she does not, she is prepared to sacrifice her own life to ensure the death of her enemies (392-4). Medea's heroic obsession with honour and revenge thus opens up a variety of potential outcomes and keeps the audience intrigued by the developing plot.

Second choral song (first *stasimon*) 410-45

The Chorus have so far been concerned to comment directly on events before them. Now, in their first full-scale choral ode,[45] they extend their range of reference and reflection more widely. They sing and dance two pairs of metrically responding stanzas:[46] the first pair criticises the unjust treatment of the female sex as a whole, while the second addresses Medea and her predicament directly. Such a movement from general reflection to a particular example is found in many choral songs (cf. the second and third stasima below). The Chorus begin by launching a daring attack on the sexual bias of the Greek poetic tradition itself (410-30), an attack that is all the more forceful for being delivered by a female Chorus. They not only offer a remarkable insight into the exclusively male control of poetic memory, but also challenge its adverse effects on women's cultural status. The limited access to story and song in Greek society is thus exposed as an instrument of women's oppression (cf. Chapter 2).

In the eyes of the Chorus, however, Jason's infidelity explodes the stereotype of female deception. The muses, female guardians of poetry, will no longer sing of women's faithlessness (421-3).[47] In the second strophic pair the Chorus turn from women's undeserved reputation to Medea's undeserved suffering. She no longer has a husband or civic rights (436-8); both her own and her father's house are closed to her (441-5). In a vivid metaphor the Chorus describe respect itself as having 'flown through the air', leaving Greece altogether, along with the reciprocity of oaths (439-40). Jason's betrayal of his oath thus takes on a more elevated moral significance and the Chorus' condemnation of his conduct could hardly be stronger.

Third scene (second *epeisodion*) 446-626

Jason enters from the direction of the royal palace in Corinth. It is no coincidence that he appears just after a powerful choral meditation on the faithlessness of men: the ordering of events makes us more alive to his imminent lies and evasions. Whereas Medea was forced to dissimulate and abase herself in her encounter with Creon, here she is utterly forthright and spares no energy in detailing Jason's shamelessness and ingratitude.

He begins by blaming Medea for her banishment: if it were not for her 'foolish words' (450, cf. 457) against the royal household, she could have stayed in Corinth. In fact, he says, she should be thankful to get away alive (454). Perhaps the most galling thing for Medea, however, is Jason's claim that he is still her 'friend' and has her best interests at heart (459-60): no matter how much she hates him, he could never wish her ill (463-4)! Jason's hypocrisy and self-deception are manifest, and when he announces that he has come to offer Medea and the children money for their exile (461-2), his 'generosity' appears grotesque (cf. 612).

Jason's opening speech provokes Medea to a lengthy and bitter response (465-519), and their meeting soon takes on the form of an *agôn* (or 'contest'):[48] Medea's speech is answered at equal length by Jason (522-75) and the scene concludes with angry dialogue (579-626). Within this simple framework, however, the characters are able to articulate the central themes and conflicts of the play. Jason has abandoned Medea and married Creon's daughter, and the purpose of each speaker is to impugn or defend this action from their own point of view. The *agôn* form thus expresses Jason and Medea's complete alienation. Appropriately, Medea begins her speech in a tone of ardent invective, attacking Jason's cowardice and shamelessness (465-72). The start of her argument is then signalled by a formal *agôn* marker: 'I shall begin my speech from the very beginning' (475).[49] By foregrounding Medea's skilful use of rhetoric, the scene reveals another side of her character, for she is capable of logical argument as well as passionate feeling. Medea's rhetorical display thereby challenges the stereotype of women as creatures of emotion rather than reason (cf. Chapter 2).

Medea's first point is that she saved Jason's life in Colchis (476-9), a substantial service, but only one of many, for she also killed the snake that guarded the Golden Fleece (480-2), betrayed her own family (483-5), and ruined the house of Pelias

(486-7). Yet despite these favours, and despite the birth of their two sons (489-91), Jason has betrayed her. Medea's response mixes argument with biting sarcasm: 'In return for these favours you've made me the envy of many Greek women! What a wonderful husband I have in my misery, and what a trusty one, if I am to be driven into exile from this land!' (509-11).

As is usual in *agônes*, a brief remark by the Chorus separates the two speeches (520-1). When Jason begins his defence, he does so with marked rhetorical self-consciousness (522-5; cf. 545-6, 548-50), but 'in this speech, in contrast to Medea's, the use of rhetoric implies the insincerity of the speaker'.[50] Using the rhetoric of Greek superiority to barbarians (cf. Chapter 3), Jason tries to claim that Medea has herself benefited by being brought to Greece (534-41). However, as the circumstances demand, Jason spends most time defending his decision to marry Creon's daughter (547-68). In this context his claim to be 'a great friend to you and my children' (549-50) is too much for Medea, whose gesture of protest is smothered by Jason's 'Be quiet now!' (550). In defence of his remarriage Jason argues that his main intention was to give his children a better future (562-5), but his rhetoric of concern rings hollow, since he has apparently made no attempt to keep the children at Corinth. Significantly, the Chorus, who generally maintain a distanced neutrality in such debates, immediately condemn Jason's use of rhetoric for an unjust cause (576-8). Medea reinforces their criticisms (579-85) and, in the bitter dialogue that follows, exposes the hypocritical secrecy of Jason's conduct.

Third choral song (second *stasimon*) 627-62

As Jason returns to the royal palace, the Chorus sing an ode which has a profound relevance to both his behaviour and the suffering it has caused Medea.[51] The first strophic pair begins with a reflection on the power of Aphrodite (627-31): 'Desires that come in excess bring neither a good name nor excellence to men. If Kypris comes in moderation, no other goddess is so gracious.' Since the last scene ended with Medea berating Jason for his submission to erotic desire (623-5), the Chorus' general remarks have a specific reference to Jason's new marriage. And when the Chorus invoke Aphrodite and pray she may never afflict them with arrows that are 'anointed with passion' (635), we inevitably think of Jason as afflicted in this way. The Chorus continue to praise 'moderation' (636) in the antistrophe, once again using words that have an implicit relevance to Jason (638-41): 'May terrible Kypris never cast quarrelsome anger and insatiable conflicts upon me, striking my heart with desire for another's bed!' As in the first stasimon (431), the second strophe begins with a direct address. The Chorus invoke their native land and home, saying they would rather die than become 'cityless' (646), and their reference to Medea is justified by autopsy (654-5): 'I have seen it, and do not report a tale I heard from others.' Though their final remark is gnomic and general, there is no doubt whom they have in mind (659-62): 'May he die unloved, the man who cannot honour his friends by unlocking an honest mind! He will never be a friend of mine.'

Fourth scene (third *epeisodion*) 663-823

Aegeus, king of Athens, enters on his way from Delphi to Troezen. Ever since Aristotle criticised the Aegeus scene for alleged illogicality (*Poetics* 1461b19-21), it has often been condemned as an example of poor plot construction, the impression being that Aegeus' entry here is somehow improbable or artificial.[52] But as one scholar points out, 'such casualness is readily acceptable to an audience provided that the scene is dramatically significant, and provided that it is seen to be part of a structural pattern.'[53] Both conditions are clearly fulfilled here: Medea has stressed her need for a place of refuge before she can proceed properly with her revenge (cf. 386-91), and a potential 'rescuer' now appears.[54] The Chorus has just lamented Medea's lack of friends (656-7), yet Aegeus' first words make clear that he and Medea are established *philoi* (663-4). The question 'Where will Medea go?' (e.g. 359, 502) may now have an answer.

The opening passage of extended stichomythia (single line dialogue) falls into two parts. Aegeus first responds to Medea's questions (666-88), then asks in turn about her welfare (689-707). The structure of the dialogue expresses their mutual respect and concern for one another, in contrast to Jason's selfish neglect of his family in the previous scene. Aegeus reports that he has been to Delphi to enquire of the oracle how he might have children. Medea's response is significant: 'In the name of the gods, are you still childless so late in life?' As in the previous scene with Jason (cf. 558-67), it is stressed how important children are to a man's identity, status, and posterity.[55] When Medea explains how she has been treated, Aegeus calls Jason 'evil' (699) and condemns him for allowing his family to go into exile (707).[56]

Once again Medea supplicates a king to achieve her purpose (709ff.), and having attained an extra day in Corinth (324ff.), she now gains a place of refuge in Athens (719-20). There is a terrible appropriateness in her use of supplication to secure Jason's punishment, for he has abused the ritual himself by not honouring the obligations which he incurred from his successful supplication of Medea in Colchis (cf. 496-8). Aegeus grants Medea her request, but imposes one condition: she must make her own way to Athens (729-30). So instead of asking 'Will Medea find a refuge?', the question for the audience now becomes 'How will she get there?', and the following scenes raise this question repeatedly, in preparation for Medea's miraculous departure (cf. 729, 757, 771, 1122-3, 1237, 1294-7). Medea has her own request: Aegeus is to swear to protect her (731-40), and by stressing the importance of Aegeus' oath and his readiness to honour it (746-55), the scene underlines both the oath-breaking of Jason and the fact that Medea is planning the kind of revenge which could bring the Corinthians to Athens demanding her surrender.[57]

Once Aegeus has left for Troezen, Medea delivers a devastating speech which crucially alters the direction of the play (764-810). Invoking Zeus and Justice, she tells the Chorus of her plans for revenge: she will deceive Jason and use their children to bring about the death of Creon's daughter (776-89).[58] But the most important part of her speech, and the turning point of the play, is Medea's shocking announcement that she will kill her own children (792-3; contrast 374-5). Not only does this fundamentally change the audience's attitude to Medea (cf. Chapter 4), it also builds suspense towards the play's horrendous climax, provoking us to wonder whether anyone can stop Medea and whether she herself can go through with such an act. It is thus one of the scene's major ironies that although Aegeus is promised children by Medea (716-18), his agreement apparently seals the death of her own sons.[59]

Fourth choral song (third *stasimon*) 824-65

As the Nurse goes off to summon Jason from the royal palace (820-3), the Chorus sing of the city of Athens and Medea's possible future there.[60] The first two stanzas hail Athens as a place of beauty, peace, and wisdom (824-45), while the second pair urges Medea not to kill her children (850-65). There is thus a great difference in both tone and content between the song's two parts, but they are linked together significantly by the opening lines of the second strophe, which ask how a child-killer like Medea could ever find refuge in such a city (846-50). The song must have had a remarkable impact upon an Athenian audience, for it begins by describing Athens and the Athenians in terms reminiscent of divine hymns. The Athenians are 'chil-

dren of the blessed gods' (825); they are 'forever stepping grace-
fully through the brilliant air' (829-30) and their land is 'sacred
and unravaged' (825-6). The previous choral song rejected excessive passion as leading to evil acts (cf. 627-9), but in Athens,
the Chorus say, Aphrodite 'has sent Desires to sit at Wisdom's
side, joint workers in every kind of excellence' (844-5). The
Athenians, in other words, blend passion and intellectual cleverness in perfect measure (cf. 830-4).

However, while it is certainly striking that a Corinthian
Chorus should praise Athens in such terms, their idealised
vision soon emerges as a foil for more disturbing reflections. The
second strophe begins by addressing Medea directly (846-50):
'How can this city of sacred rivers or this country that gives safe
escort to friends accept you, the killer of your children, the
unholy one, to live among them?' The purpose of the Chorus'
extensive praise of Athens is now clear: they mean to avert
Medea's infanticide by persuading her that such a city would
never take her in. Yet the audience know that Athens is already
bound by Aegeus' oath to accept Medea and that Aegeus' agreement will nearly destroy his own son Theseus, Athens' greatest
hero. While this may be seen as critical of Medea's cunning
rather than Aegeus' generosity, the Chorus' question does at
least complicate the vision of Athens as a perfect and peaceful
community. The Chorus plead repeatedly with Medea not to
dare such a crime, even supplicating her (853-5) and envisaging
a supplication by her terrified children as well (862-5). However,
unlike Medea's acts of supplication, those of the Chorus and her
children are in vain.

Fifth scene (fourth *epeisodion*) 866-975

Jason re-enters from the royal palace, accompanied by the
Nurse. The scene abounds in significant effects of parallelism
and contrast with Medea and Jason's previous encounter (446-

626). In their first meeting we saw the authentic Medea, raging at Jason's betrayal. Here, however, following the crucial Aegeus episode and with her revenge plan underway, Medea disguises her true feelings and becomes the very model of submissive femininity preferred by Jason (cf. Chapter 2). Since Medea has already made clear the true nature of her plans (cf. 772-97), we are prepared for the multiple ironies of their meeting, as Jason is led to believe that Medea has given up her anger and so becomes an unwitting accomplice in his own ruin.

Medea begins by begging Jason's forgiveness and endorses his arguments in favour of his new marriage (869-81). She calls the children (with the Paidagogos) from the house (894-5); their presence is appropriate to the scene of 'reconciliation' being staged by Medea, but it also echoes the opening scene of the play (cf. 46-110): the prologue's forebodings about the children's safety are about to be given concrete expression. When she is reminded of Jason's treachery, Medea laments 'some hidden sorrow' which may befall their sons (899-900), but neither Jason nor the children can understand the threatening ambiguity of her remarks (cf. 925, 930-1, 974-5). Suddenly, Medea breaks down in tears (922-4) and her emotions create suspense: will she be able to go through with the murder? Jason, by contrast, remains unbearably patronising (cf. 908-13); ironically, his address to, and sudden interest in, his sons comes just as he is about to lose them (914-21). Yet the final irony of the scene is perhaps the harshest: Medea prepares to destroy Jason's new wife using his own children (946-58). As the children go off with the poisoned wedding gifts, Medea instructs them to beg Creon's daughter for a reprieve from exile: once again Medea uses supplication to further her revenge (971).

37

Fifth choral song (fourth *stasimon*) 976-1001

As Jason returns to the royal palace, accompanied by the children and the Paidagogos, the Chorus envisage the deaths awaiting both Creon's daughter and the children. Whereas the children are described simply and powerfully as 'already walking towards a bloody death' (977), the destruction of Creon's daughter is pictured at greater length, foreshadowing the messenger's gory details in the following scene. The song is much shorter than the first three stasima and lacks their passages of general reflection, creating greater pace and a more intense focus on the imminent deaths. In the first strophic pair the Chorus imagine Creon's daughter transformed by the wedding gifts into a bride of Hades (980-5). The perversion of marriage ritual marks the impending ruin of both Jason and Creon's households. The second strophe begins by addressing Jason directly. Significantly, the Chorus now express some sympathy for him (995): 'Unhappy man, how little you know of your fate!' Yet despite their sympathy, the Chorus make clear that they consider Jason jointly responsible for the death of his sons (cf. 992-3), for he has abandoned Medea 'lawlessly' (1000-1).

Sixth scene (fifth *epeisodion*) 1002-250

The Paidagogos returns from the palace with the children, who thus reappear immediately after a choral song about their murder. The Paidagogos happily reports that Creon's daughter has accepted the gifts, yet he cannot understand Medea's miserable reaction to the news. As she sends him into the house 'to attend to the children's daily needs' (1019-20), the audience can appreciate the poignancy of her command. Medea is left alone on stage with her children.[61] Her series of confrontations now culminates in a struggle with herself, and in a long and harrowing monologue she faces her maternal grief at the intended murder. Twice she declares that she cannot kill the children (1044-8, 1056-8), but each time fear of her enemies' laughter reasserts itself and compels her to take revenge.[62]

Medea sends the children into the house (1076). At each of their earlier exits (cf. 105, 974-5) there was some doubt as to whether they would be seen again, but here our fears for their lives are most acute. Euripides deliberately draws out the suspense by placing a long passage of choral anapaests (1081-115) and an extended messenger speech (1136-230) between the children's departure and Medea's exit after them into the house (1250). Medea is keen to relish the horrific details of her revenge (1133-4): 'But do not hurry, my friend: tell your story!' The Messenger, by contrast, is shocked at her triumphant reaction (cf. 1129-31). Nearly all of Euripides' surviving tragedies contain at least one messenger speech (the sole exception is *Trojan Women*). Here the Messenger is a slave who once worked in Medea's household, but now belongs to Jason's new *oikos* within the royal palace (cf. 1144-5). The subject of his speech, the death of Creon's daughter, has already been well prepared for (cf. 774-89, 947-75, 978-88, 1002-4, 1065-6), but here we get a lavish eye-witness description of the event itself.

The Messenger begins by describing how happy he and the others slaves were at the sight of the children in the palace, since they took this as evidence of Medea and Jason's reconciliation (1136-42). By contrast, Jason's new wife is disgusted by their arrival and veils her face (1147-9). Though the Messenger quotes a short cajoling speech by Jason, the narrative makes clear that it is the gifts which Creon's daughter actually finds persuasive (1149-57). She cannot resist their beauty and puts them on as soon as Jason and the children leave. In a significant moment of plot prolepsis, the Messenger describes the young woman admiring herself in a mirror, 'smiling at the *lifeless* reflection of her body' (1162). The scene effectively conveys both her vanity and her deluded happiness (cf. 1163-6).

39

The Messenger's account of her death is exceptionally gruesome. The poisoned robe and crown devour the woman's flesh
and set her head on fire. Only a parent, the Messenger says,
could have recognised her corpse (1196), preparing us for
Creon's sudden arrival. Touching his daughter's corpse (as the
Messenger and the other slaves present were afraid to do:
1202-3), he too is infected by the poison, and his mournful wish,
'Alas, may I die with you, dear child!' (1210), is immediately
realised, as the flesh is torn from his bones. Creon's agony
foreshadows Jason's impending loss of his own children. Indeed,
as the Messenger returns to the palace, the Chorus remark that
'Heaven seems this day to be *justly* fastening many disasters
upon Jason' (1231-2). So once again, despite their condemnation
of Medea's impending infanticide, the Chorus hold Jason responsible for what has happened. Before her final exit into the
house, Medea delivers a short and urgent speech which reasserts her determination to kill her children (1236-50). Because
Medea has been on stage since the start of the first episode
(214), dominating the other characters and preparing her revenge, her eventual exit has a powerful dramatic impact, which
is made all the stronger by her brutal purpose within.

Sixth choral song (fifth *stasimon*) 1251-92

As Medea goes into the house, the Chorus appeal for the murder
to be prevented. They sing in dochmiacs, an excited metre that
expresses their emotional turmoil.[63] The pattern of aeolo-
choriambic metres found in the first four stasima is thus broken, marking the Chorus' shocked response to the imminent
murder of the children. They begin by calling on Earth and
Helios to intervene on the children's behalf. Helios, Medea's
grandfather, is asked to save the descendants of his 'golden race'
(1255). However, since Helios will actually help Medea escape
(1321-2), the Chorus' prayer points forward to the troubling

aspects of his collaboration. In the antistrophe the Chorus turn to Medea, lamenting her wasted efforts to bear and rear her children (1261-2). They warn her that the shedding of kindred blood causes pollution and divine punishment (1268-70). Once again the Chorus' conventional piety prepares for the play's shocking finale, where Medea appears as an agent of divine punishment herself (cf. Chapter 4).

As the infanticide approaches, a scream is heard from inside the house (1270a), and the play 'achieves its most powerful climax of violence by having the child's cry break into what begins and ends as a regular choral ode'.[64] We then hear the offstage iambic dialogue of the two children as they try to escape death:[65] 'Oh no! What can I do? How can I escape my mother's hands?' / 'I don't know, dearest brother! We're destroyed!' (1271-2). The Chorus acknowledge that they should go into the house to intervene (1275-6). By challenging the convention that keeps the tragic chorus on stage, the Chorus' reaction marks the peculiar horror of the murder, but also their own powerlessness to stop it. These feelings are intensified when the children respond directly to the Chorus, creating an exceptional and poignant dialogue between the stage and offstage area: 'Yes, in heaven's name, protect us! We need you!' / 'How close we now are to the sword's snare!' (1277-8). Significantly, the iambics of the antistrophe are spoken not by the children, but by the Chorus (1284-5, 1288-9): 'The silence of those responding voices ... is a dramatically powerful indication of what has taken place inside the house.'[66] Rather than intervene directly, the Chorus recall the story of Ino, who killed her own children, but was punished by a death at sea. The mythical parallel thus suggests that Medea too may die for her horrendous act, an expectation which is powerfully undone in the final scene.

41

Seventh and final scene (*exodos*) 1293-419

Jason enters hurriedly from the direction of the palace and immediately asks the Chorus if Medea is still inside the house. If she is to escape punishment, Jason says, 'She must either hide herself beneath the earth or soar on wings into the heights of the sky' (1296-7). His words are a conventional expression of the impossibility of escape (cf. *Hippolytus* 1290-3, *Heracles* 1157-8, *Ion* 1238-9), but here they prepare for the miraculous and superhuman nature of Medea's final exit. Jason has come to save his sons from the vengeance of the royal family (1301-5); the allusion to a more familiar (and less shocking) version of the myth (cf. 781-2, 1238-9, 1380-1) underlines the terrible climax of the play: it never occurs to Jason that Medea may kill the children herself. When the Chorus warn him that he faces much greater misfortune, his first reaction is typically to think of himself: 'What is it? Does she mean to kill me as well?' (1308).

The Chorus reveal the truth: 'Open the doors and you will see your children's bloody murder' (1313). Jason orders the servants inside the house to release the bolts (1314-15). The attention of the audience is thus fixed on the centre of the *skênê* and they are led to expect that the doors will open to reveal Medea and the corpses on the *ekkyklêma* (or 'rolling-out platform'). But in a spectacular and powerful moment of theatrical misdirection, Euripides has Medea appear with the bodies above the *skênê*, carried in a flying chariot that rises from behind the house.[67] Thus one dramatic convention (the *ekkyklêma*-scene) is disrupted and replaced surprisingly by another, the *deus ex machina* (or 'god from the machine'). Medea's opening words express her new status: elevated in more than a merely physical sense, she speaks to Jason with superhuman authority, ordering him to leave the doors alone (1317-19).

Jason's reply is furious and hateful: he calls Medea a traitor to her family and country (1332), something she had herself regretted earlier (cf. 166-7, 483-5, 502-3), and he deplores the murder of her brother Apsyrtus (1333-5), even though he was happy enough to profit from it at the time. To the very last Jason refuses to accept his part in the disaster. Instead he merely reproduces the same stereotypes that have already been challenged in their earlier meetings, attacking Medea as a sex-obsessed woman and dangerous foreigner (1338-40). Nor can he accept the part played by the gods in his ruin: although Helios has supplied Medea with the chariot for her escape (1321-2), Jason presumes that the god could not bear to look upon her pollution (1327-8). Seeing his dead sons, he laments 'I shall never be able to speak to my children alive, the ones I begot and nurtured, but have lost them' (1349-50), yet his final word *apôlesa* ('I have lost them') can also mean 'I have destroyed them', creating an ambiguity which the audience can appreciate, despite Jason's unwillingness to admit his own share of responsibility.

Refusing the opportunity to respond to Jason at length,[68] Medea claims divine approval for her revenge (1351-3). In bitter stichomythia (a form of dialogue where each speaker delivers a single line) she and Jason blame each other for the death of the children (1361-73). When Jason asks for the bodies so that he can bury them, Medea denies him even this ritual consolation, and her speech marks her new god-like status, as she establishes a Corinthian cult to atone for the murder of her children and predicts Jason's shameful death (1378-88). The metre changes to anapaests for the closing lines of the play: both the metre and the pain-filled cries of Jason recall the opening scene, where Medea sang in anapaests from inside the house. Here, however, the roles are reversed and it is Jason who calls on the gods to witness his ill-treatment (1405-10). Though he finally shows affection for his children and begs to be allowed to touch them (1399-400, 1402-3), Medea remains aloof, pitiless, and exultant in her revenge. As she disappears in her chariot with the bodies of her children, bound first for the shrine of Hera Akraia (1378-9) and then for Athens (1384-5), the Chorus leave the *orchêstra* with a final reflection on the gods' power to bring about the unexpected (1415-19).[69]

At the level of plot *Medea* could hardly be called a complex play and yet its power to move and shock audiences is indisputable. Our discussion of the play's structure and stagecraft has tried to show how Euripides achieves these powerful effects, especially through his use of dramatic irony, emotional suspense, and disturbing violence. If we look back at the development of the action, we see an intense focus on Medea, her sense of dishonour, and her reaction to it. She stands at the centre of a series of confrontations (with the Chorus, Creon, Aegeus, and Jason), each of which she dominates by a combination of rhetorical brilliance, emotional manipulation, and skilled deception. Medea can play the pathetic or apologetic woman if it will further her plans (cf. 230-66, 869-905), but beneath her various personae lies a coherent, credible, and effective character, a woman with a strong sense of honour and justice whose suffering and humiliation drive her to revenge. However, Medea's decision to react as she does is complicated and enriched by her status as a woman, a foreigner, and a not quite mortal avenger. Therefore the aim of the following three chapters is to investigate these aspects of her role in greater detail. Finally, since *Medea* has had such an exceptionally productive and dynamic reception, Chapter 5 considers some of the reinterpretations and adaptations which have been produced in response to Euripides' work, and argues that, while they clearly illustrate specific contemporary concerns, these later works can also throw new light back onto Euripides' original play.

2

Husbands and Wives

Greek tragedy, and Euripidean tragedy in particular, is profoundly concerned with problems and conflicts of gender, yet in
no other play has Euripides presented such a powerful and
subversive female figure as Medea or such a radical critique of
male tradition and authority. The aim of this chapter is to
discuss the key issues of gender which are raised in the play and
to relate these to the society of its original audience. In general
terms, given that tragedy characteristically addresses tensions
inherent in Athenian society, its repeated engagement with
gender is not surprising, for the relative status and expected
roles of men and women have been, and remain, issues of debate
and potential conflict in most human communities.[1]

Nevertheless, the frequency with which such issues are
raised in tragedy is striking, and the reasons for this lie in the
nature of both the genre and Athenian society itself. As drama
the tragedies are powered by human interaction, generally
between male and female characters,[2] and the myths upon
which the plays are based frequently involve gender conflict. In
addition, Athenian society was marked by firm divisions between the sexes and multiple constraints upon the possibilities
of female agency and authority. As a result of these factors, both
generic and social, the tensions which the tragedies explore
were sure to engage the convictions and anxieties of their
original audience. Moreover, it is important to consider the
composition of the audience itself, for the presence of women,
which seems on balance more likely than their absence,[3] must

have widened the range of response to the disturbing and even radical questions of sexual politics which are raised by the plays.[4]

When we look at the characters and plots of the surviving plays, it is clear that Euripides was not the only dramatist to see the relative status of the sexes as a powerful dramatic catalyst. Clytemnestra and the Danaids (Aeschylus, *Oresteia, Suppliant Women*), for example, or Deianeira, Antigone, and Electra (Sophocles, *Women of Trachis, Antigone, Electra*), are figures whose suffering and response are shown to be closely tied to their roles and powers as women. Yet it was Euripides who raised issues of gender conflict most insistently and gave women and their concerns greater prominence in his plays. Most of his seventeen surviving tragedies have female leading roles (*Alcestis, Medea, Hippolytus, Andromache, Hecuba, Electra, Trojan Women, Iphigenia in Tauris, Ion, Helen, Phoenician Women, Orestes, Iphigenia in Aulis*) and all but three (*Alcestis, Heraclidae, Heracles*) have female choruses, while his earliest extant work, the pro-satyric *Alcestis*,[5] calls into question the model of the self-sacrificing wife, and neither its pro-satyric atmosphere nor its happy ending dull the play's disruptive impact.

Throughout his career Euripides' plays are not only more insistent than those of his predecessors in their analysis of women's status, but also more overt, topical, and controversial in their challenge to the dominant sexual ideology of fifth-century Athens. It is a measure of his striking effects in this area that although Euripides was not alone in presenting transgressive women on the tragic stage, Aristophanes chose to mock him as a misogynist (e.g. Aristophanes, *Women at the Thesmophoria* 372-465). Aristophanes' criticisms are an essentially parodic reaction to Euripides' intense portrayal of female suffering and revenge, but beneath the comic burlesque his jokes suggest that the female figures of Euripides had a particularly strong impact on the Athenian audience. *Medea* shows clearly why this was so, for it explores the experience of an intelligent and articulate woman in a society which denied women such attributes. Euripides has transformed the Medea myth so that it exposes many of the inequalities underlying the status of real women. A play set in mythical Corinth is thus able to challenge the conventional (i.e. male) view of women's 'proper' role in contemporary Athens.

In recent years the application of feminist literary theory to Attic tragedy has raised a number of important questions. To what extent, for example, does tragedy represent gender identities that already exist in fifth-century Athenian society? To what extent does it support them? Is tragedy a tool of patriarchal repression or does it subvert such male-driven ideology? On the whole, feminist criticism tends to see tragedy (and literature generally) as legitimating the power structures of Athenian society. Thus one scholar argues that tragedy portrays 'the disastrous effects on households and the larger community of ... women unsupervised by men'.[6] In other words, the plays warn the male audience of the dangers inherent in allowing women too much independence. In *Medea*, however, the issue of 'supervision' is not stressed: it is Jason who has freely chosen to abandon his wife for a more advantageous marriage.

Another recent approach is to see the female characters themselves as mere ciphers for the exploration of male conduct and identity: 'in Greek theater ... the self that is really at stake is to be identified with the male, while the woman is assigned the role of the radical other .... *Functionally* women are never an end in themselves, and nothing changes for them once they have lived out their drama onstage.'[7] Yet Medea's life is radically altered by events on stage and the play focuses on her suffering and response as a woman just as much as it does on Jason's (unsatisfactory) conduct as a man. To interpret tragedy in terms of a 'male self' on display does not do justice to the plays, while it presents a rather narrow view of the 'constructed' audience as well: even if only the men in the theatre can be said to constitute the primary audience, there is no reason why they might not find the female figures on stage interesting in their own right. Moreover, it would be implausible to postulate a single monolithic 'male' response to the events and characters of a play. The situation was more complex: different viewers will have responded in different ways. Where one saw merely confirmation of his misogynistic and paternalistic opinions (as in Medea's vengeful murder of her own children), another may have been provoked by Medea's complaints to reflect more deeply on the gender(ed) inequalities of Athenian society.[8]

So rather than seeing tragedy as a series of cautionary tales for male conduct or as a reinforcement of the dominant sexual ideology, it may be more profitable to take the social values of fifth-century Athens as a base and then consider how a genre set in the world of heroic myth engages with and explores these values without necessarily endorsing them. Tragedy presents various models of masculinity and femininity, but rather than simply asserting one over the other, it exposes their problems and the tensions between them. At the most basic level, tragedy cannot be said simply to uphold male structures of authority when it frequently presents the straitened circumstances of women's lives in such an affecting way as to suggest that both their treatment and their allotted status and roles are unacceptable. This is not to say that *Medea* is a feminist drama in any simple sense, for Medea is a complex and ambiguous figure. Yet tragedy in general, and *Medea* in particular, is more exploratory and critical of established values than it is supportive of women's prescribed roles of domesticity and silence.[9]

As has been observed, recent scholarship has 'shifted the focus from recovering women's historical reality to understanding the conceptual framework behind their literary and mythic representation and relating it to the social and ideological context of democratic Athens'.[10] But these two projects (historical and representational) are inseparable, and we must attempt to recover women's history, despite the bias of the sources, rather than merely settle for a model that sees male hegemony being reinforced at every turn. So what was the status of women in fifth-century Athens? There is no simple or single answer: it depends on both the arena in question (politics, law, religion, *oikos*, myth, etc.) and the social class of the women concerned. In terms of spatial seclusion, for example, with women 'ideally' confined to their own quarters within the house, such an absolute division between inside and outside cannot have been rigorously maintained by poorer women, since they had to go out to work.[11] Nevertheless, it may be that poorer people themselves viewed the values of the rich as to some extent normative, in which case the division (referred to in the royal households of tragedy) between male / *polis* and female / *oikos* space will have had some meaning for poorer audience members as well.

In one sense, of course, all women, regardless of their socio-economic class, were marginal members of the Athenian *polis*, for they played no role in its public political life, being forbidden from participation in the Assembly and the law-courts. Indeed, in legal matters a woman was 'a perpetual minor ... almost in law an un-person'.[12] Yet against this relative lack of power and self-determination must be set women's important role as mothers, that is, as bearers of the male citizen-soldiers who would ensure the city's future security and survival. Moreover, the new citizenship law proposed by Pericles in 451/0 BC decreed that a man could only be a citizen if both his parents were Athenian. Athenian women were thus essential to the continuity of the citizen elite through the production of legitimate heirs.[13] No less fundamental were their roles in the day-to-day economic life of the *oikos* and the religious life of both the household and the city. Religion was a major sphere of female status and power: 'the traditional and pervasive involvement of women in Athenian cult ... is an important corrective to the simple polarities, "man / woman : public / private" and "man / woman : citizen / non-citizen".'[14] Women thus differed crucially from barbarians (cf. Chapter 3) in that they were *polis* 'insiders', albeit ones barred from the 'democratic' political system of men.[15]

Gender is presented as a source of conflict in almost every scene and song of *Medea*. As contrasting views of the sexes are expressed by the figures on stage, the audience can evaluate and respond to them. Many other factors may affect their estimation of the characters, but none is handled more persistently throughout the play than the status and proper roles of men and women. In her opening monologue the Nurse contrasts Medea and Jason's former harmony with their present disaffection. Medea left Iolcus 'struck in her heart with desire for Jason' (8), and when they reached Corinth, 'she pleased him in every way' (13). Yet Medea's passionate love and dutiful devotion have been undone by Jason's treachery. The Nurse's language, like her moral contrast between husband and wife, is direct and powerful (16-19):

> But now all's hatred and the dearest bonds are sick. For Jason has betrayed his own sons and my mistress, bedding down in a royal marriage with the daughter of Creon, who rules this land.

In other plays Euripides presents the passion of an adulterous wife (e.g. *Sthenoboea, Phoenix, Peleus, Hippolytus* I and II). Medea, by contrast, is presented as passionately devoted to her husband, and it is Jason who has destroyed their marriage by taking another partner. In the heroic world of the play Medea is Jason's legitimate wife and his behaviour cannot be excused as if he were abandoning (in fifth-century terms) a mere foreign *pallakê* (or 'concubine'): 'The essential situation is perfectly clear-cut: Jason and Medea are to be regarded as permanently pledged, so that when Jason abandons Medea he *is* breaking faith (and even he does not deny it).'[16] The 'dearest bonds of *philia*' (16) encompass not only their marriage and children, the physical embodiment of their pledge, but also the ties of friendship and favour owed by Jason to Medea because of her help in securing the Golden Fleece (e.g. the murder of Pelias, 9-10). Thus the Nurse can describe Jason's action as a 'betrayal' (17) and her sympathetic description of the situation leads us to believe that Medea is justified in feeling dishonoured (cf. 20, 33).

The Nurse's speech also raises the issue of divine anger, which is important for our understanding of the play and particularly its last scene. For in addition to disrespecting Medea's standing in the *oikos*, Jason has violated the universal religious obligation of oaths. The Nurse depicts Medea's misery and inconsolable rage within the house as she invokes the gods to witness Jason's breach of trust (21-3). And Medea, spurned by her husband, now laments her own 'betrayal' of her native land by coming to Greece with Jason (31-2). The Nurse thus underlines the transgressive nature of Medea's marriage, which was made without the consent of her father (cf. Pindar, *Olympian* 13.53) and in circumstances which led to her total isolation from her family. Insofar as a bride would normally leave her natal *oikos* for that of her husband, but still retain links with the former, Medea's transgressive marriage meant an exclusive bond to Jason's *oikos*, which he has now destroyed. Thus Medea's peculiarly dependent marital status compounds her sense of abandonment and hurt.

Whereas the Nurse's opening speech foregrounds Medea's own response to her maltreatment, the dialogue that follows between the Nurse and the Paidagogos presents the turmoil inside the house from a more detached viewpoint. Significantly, however, the reaction of the slaves confirms Medea's sense of injustice. The Paidagogos' concern naturally centres on Medea and Jason's children, as he reports the rumour that Creon means to banish them from Corinth along with their mother (67-73). The Nurse is shocked that Jason should stand by and let his sons be treated in such a way; his inaction proves him a bad father (82-4). The Paidagodos agrees and criticises Jason for neglecting his paternal duties and no longer loving his sons 'for the sake of a bed' (88). Such criticisms make it difficult for the audience simply to accept Jason's argument that he remarried for the sake of his sons, not for his own profit or ambition (cf. 559-65, 595-7).

In addition to the Nurse and Paidagogos, the opening of the play introduces another voice sympathetic to Medea's plight, that of the Chorus of Corinthian women. As in other plays of Euripides (*Hippolytus, Andromache, Electra, Orestes*), the Chorus is composed of free local women who are sympathetic to the plight of the protagonist. As P.E. Easterling observes, 'the scenario is ... that of a shared women's world'.[17] The gender of the Chorus crucially affects the development of the play's key themes and it is hard to imagine any of their songs being sung by a Chorus of Corinthian men. They are dismayed by Medea's suffering and stress that they come in friendship (cf. 138, 179, 181). Yet their advice is quietist and conventional: Medea should not be angry with Jason; Zeus will advocate her cause (155-7). As average women they cannot conceive of taking matters into their own hands and their response throws into greater prominence Medea's unconventional decision to punish Jason herself.

When Medea finally comes out to address the Chorus (214ff.), her demeanour is very unlike the tearful and despairing figure so far described by the Nurse or heard screaming from inside the house (cf. 24-33, 96-7, 111-14, 144-7, 160-7). Instead her speech is calm and rational as she explains her situation to the Chorus and appeals for their support. Indeed, so marked is the contrast that several scholars have viewed it as a problem: 'If we believe in a woman as distraught as the Medea of the prologue, we find it hard to believe that she will so quickly turn into the crafty tactician of the following scene. If we believe in the intriguer, there does not seem to be room there for the wailing wife.'[18] Yet this so-called conflict only arises if one assumes too static a picture of dramatic characterisation.[19] Medea is indeed presented in a variety of states, angry and distraught at one moment, controlled and reasoning the next, but the contrast is emotionally plausible and the audience find it credible and persuasive rather than problematic.[20]

In her opening words Medea justifies her decision to leave the house, the primary sphere of a woman's life, in order publicly to defend her sense of injustice. Yet although her movement and purpose are culturally coded as 'masculine', she speaks to the female Chorus of the miseries of womanhood, looking beyond her own personal betrayal by Jason (225-9) to their shared disadvantages as women in order to win the Chorus' sympathy and support.[21] Beginning 'Of all creatures who have life and thought we women are the most wretched', Medea's description of constrained female experience (230-51) is unsurpassed in Greek literature. She begins by complaining that women 'must pay an exorbitant price to buy a husband and take a master over our bodies' (232-4). She thus connects the dowry, a sum of money or property provided by the bride's family, with the idea of being sold into slavery, so that instead of securing her a husband the dowry merely buys her a 'master'. It would harm Medea's rhetorical purpose to mention the positive aspects of the dowry system and so she neglects them,[22] just as she elides the major differences in status between wives and slaves. But her comparison, however tendentious, captures the fundamental inequalities between men and women within marriage. For, as she points out, 'divorce ruins a woman's reputation and it is not possible to refuse her husband' (236-7). In other words, even if a woman is dissatisfied with her marriage, the disgrace of divorce (as well as her economic and social dependence) hinders her leaving, and as long as they are married, a wife cannot deny her husband's sexual demands. The husband is therefore 'master over our bodies' in the most basic sense, and Greek law did not recognise such a crime as marital rape.

Such inequalities are part of marriage from the very beginning, for as Medea observes, the new bride must adapt to the unfamiliar habits and customs of her husband's *oikos* (238-40). We must also bear in mind that girls generally married young (upon reaching puberty) and often to men at least twice their age, so that a bride was not only isolated from her peers but also relatively immature. Medea's great insight is to see that all women enter their husband's homes as outsiders. And although this is especially true of herself, a foreigner from Colchis, she speaks here as one whose experience mirrors that of her female Greek audience, the Chorus. They too can recognise the double standard at the heart of sexual morality (244-7):

> Whenever a man is dissatisfied with the company at home,
> he goes outside and rids his heart of sickness [by turning
> to some male friend or contemporary]; but it is necessary
> for us to look to one person alone.

The relief the husband seeks is evidently sexual, despite the moralising interpolation of 246, which seeks to remove the erotic force of the previous line. Extra-marital sex was always an option for men, but never for women, and Medea's simple observation exposes the male hypocrisy behind this. Her catalogue of injustice culminates in a remarkably powerful challenge to the dominant *polis* ideology of the male citizen-soldier, for Medea not only compares fighting in war to giving birth, but asserts that the latter is more dangerous (250-1): 'I would rather stand three times behind the shield than give birth once.'

By implying that childbirth represents a more hazardous, heroic, and therefore praiseworthy service to the city than hoplite-
fighting, Medea's claim constitutes a fundamental realignment
of conventional gender roles which must have shocked the
largely male Athenian audience.

So far Medea has stressed how much she and the Corinthian
Chorus have in common. In the final part of her speech, however, she draws a distinction between their rooted and secure
life and her own existence without city or family. Yet there is a
certain amount of special pleading in her claims which alerts
the audience to the complexity of Medea's portrayal: she is no
purely innocent victim. For although she describes herself as
'plundered' from her homeland by Jason (256), the audience
know that she left willingly.[23] And when she laments patheti-
cally that she has 'no mother, no brother, no relative' with whom
to seek refuge (257), the audience will recall that Medea killed
her own brother to facilitate her escape with Jason (166-7).
Nevertheless, despite her misleading rhetoric, Medea's speech
has an overwhelmingly expansive impact, for it leads the
largely male audience to see events from a female point of view.
As one scholar puts it, 'there is *involvement* with female
choices',[24] and the audience are encouraged to appreciate
women's dilemmas and injustices in their own right.

Medea's rhetorical virtuosity is but one aspect of her exceptional *sophia* (or 'cleverness'). The word *sophia* ('wisdom,
cleverness') is ambiguous, but it is regularly figured as threatening or dangerous in a woman (cf. *Hippolytus* 640-4).[25] As her
encounter with Creon shows, Medea's *sophia* arouses particular
anxiety because it is linked to her expertise in poisons and
magic.[26] Thus Creon justifies his concern for his daughter's
safety by saying, 'You are clever and skilled in many evils' (285).
In her reply Medea tries to allay Creon's suspicions by claiming
that her reputation for cleverness has only done her harm and
that it is in any case undeserved (292-305). While Medea speaks

in general of the unhappy fate of the clever citizen (cf. *Electra* 294-6), the context also suggests 'the complaint of a woman of great intellectual capacity who finds herself excluded from the spheres of power and action'.[27]

Nevertheless, Medea's (ironically subtle) disavowal of *sophia* does not convince Creon, who continues to fear her as a 'clever, silent woman' (320). He rejects her initial appeal as a suppliant not to be exiled (324-9), but accepts her second request for one day's grace (340). Medea prevails upon Creon by arousing pity for her sons (344), and there is further irony insofar as Jason's poor conduct as a father (342-3) leads to the death of Creon and his daughter, whom Creon, an exemplary father, loves most of all (cf. 329). Though he recognises his mistake, Creon agrees to Medea's request in the belief that she can do his family no harm in a single day. Yet despite his parting threat of execution, the audience know that it is Medea who has won a crucial battle in her plan for revenge,[28] and this is confirmed by her abrupt change of tone from fawning humility to scheming determination (366-7): 'There are still struggles in store for the newly-weds and for their relatives troubles that are not small.' Medea confesses proudly to her deception of Creon and considers carefully how she might kill her enemies, rejecting fire and the sword in favour of poison, seen as the archetypally 'feminine' weapon because of its cunning and secrecy (cf. 384-5). As she urges herself on to 'plan and scheme' (402, punning on her own name, which can also mean 'contriver'), Medea's 'feminine' craftiness is combined with a heroic (i.e. 'masculine') concern to avoid the laughter of her enemies (404-5).[29] While it is true that 'there is a discernible "masculinisation" of women in Greek tragedy',[30] women who act independently need not be seen by the audience as 'unfeminine' or 'dangerous', even if that is how male characters describe them (cf. e.g. Sophocles, *Antigone* 578-9). Much depends on the dramatic circumstances and the choices made by the characters. So here, in the context of

Jason's betrayal of his *oikos*, Medea's heroic concern for honour and revenge is from a certain perspective admirable and many in the audience may have been surprised to find themselves largely in sympathy with Medea's 'unfeminine' conduct.

Medea's betrayal by Jason and her audacious revenge are put into a wider context by the Chorus' first stasimon. The first strophic pair forcefully repudiate women's reputation for faithlessness: 'it is men whose plans are deceitful' (412). The Chorus joyfully predict the reversal of such stereotypes when the deceptiveness of men has been exposed (415-20):

> But the tales people tell will turn my life around so that it has a fair name. Honour is coming to the female sex! No longer will women be gripped by slanderous tales.

Yet the song is made all the more powerful by its insight into the male poetic tradition itself. For as the Chorus show, it is precisely male control of the resources of poetic memory which has shaped women's poor reputation.[31] The audience may recall the familiar declarations of female deceitfulness from Hesiod, Semonides, and other male poets, yet the Chorus assert that songs of a very different tenor would have been composed had women enjoyed equal access to poetry (421-8):

> The Muses of ancient poets will cease to sing of my faithlessness. For Phoebus, lord of poetry, did not grant our minds the lyre's inspired song; else I would have rung out a song in answer to the male sex.

The Chorus overlook the few female poets of early Greek literature in order to stress men's near exclusive control over poetic expression.[32] This is a strikingly overt and critical engagement with the poetic past, made more forceful because tragedy is shaped by it as well. The dominant literary culture of Greece is suddenly seen from an unfamiliar (female) point of view and the criticism is arresting. The fairness of the Chorus' appraisal is highlighted by their even-handed judgement of both sexes (429-30): 'Time in its long expanse has much to tell of men's lot as well as of ours.'[33] Of course, Medea has just shown herself to be a skilled deceiver (cf. 368-70), so the situation is more complex than a simple feminist interpretation might have it, but this does not annul the powerful challenge to male poetic culture made by the Chorus' song.

Moreover, the Chorus' strong expression of sympathy for Medea's plight in the second half of the ode (431-45) prepares the audience for Jason's entry. Their final stanza has just stressed Jason's appalling breach of trust ('The grace of oaths has fled', 439), so that the moralising tone of his opening words seems particularly obnoxious. Jason has come to offer Medea and the children money for their exile, and he implies that they should be grateful for his support (459-63). Significantly, his very first move is an attempt to shift the blame for Medea's exile away from himself: it is all due to Medea's 'foolish words' against the royal family (448-50). Although he claims that he tried his utmost to intercede with Creon on Medea's behalf (455-6), the audience may doubt this. After all, according to the Paidagogos (cf. 74-7, 82-8), he made little effort to thwart the banishment even of his sons. As Jason tries to present himself as Medea's loyal friend, his sanctimonious tone becomes unbearable ('Even if you hate me, I could never wish you anything bad', 463-4) and it is understandable that Medea should burst into a speech of passionate denunciation (465-519).[34]

Yet Medea's speech is important not merely for its emotional power; it also fills in much of the background to her relationship with Jason and so helps us understand her overwhelming sense of betrayal. For, as Medea says, Jason owes all his success to her support (476-7): 'I saved you, as all the Greeks know who embarked with you on that same ship, the *Argo*.' Not only did

2. Husbands and Wives

Medea help Jason to yoke her father's fire-breathing bulls and defeat the warriors who sprang up from the earth, but she herself killed the snake that protected the Golden Fleece (477-82; the crucial word *kteinasa* ('I killed') is delayed and put in an emphatic position as first word in the line). Such a revelation diminishes Jason's heroic stature still further and confirms Medea's contempt for his 'unmanliness' (cf. 466). At the same time the recollection of her powerful and independent past enhances the injustice of Medea's current predicament.[35] Moreover, as Medea points out, Jason has no good reason to seek another marriage, since she has already provided him with sons (490-1): 'If you were still childless, your desire for this marriage could be forgiven.' In other words, since Medea has fulfilled her part of the marriage contract, she deserves some measure of loyalty from Jason.[36]

In his reply Jason confronts this charge of abandonment directly, but his argument is unconvincing. For he makes his children by Medea the very reason for his new marriage (562-7):

> [I remarried] so that I might raise my children in a manner worthy of my house and, by begetting brothers for my children by you, might bind them together into one family and so be prosperous. For what need do you have of further children? But it is to my advantage to benefit those already alive by having other children in the future.

Jason envisions two *oikoi* brought together as a single unit, with his children by Medea becoming half-brothers to his new sons, the legitimate heirs to the kingdom of Corinth. Yet such a plan would seem implausible to a Greek audience, who were well aware of the possible jealousies and rivalries between legitimate and illegitimate siblings or between children and stepmothers (cf. 1147-53, *Alcestis* 304-10, 371-3, *Hippolytus* 305-10, *Andromache* 464-70), tensions which were only exacerbated if the situation also involved the inheritance of royal power. While Jason's avowed concern for his children's future may seem admirable, his aim of two households fused together is in context no more than a 'meaningless utopia of a happy future'.[37]

It has been argued that the (male) audience would find Jason's argument reasonable here on the grounds that Medea is (in fifth-century Athenian terms) a mere foreign concubine whose children would be inferior in status to those of his new marriage.[38] However, while it is true that the pre-legal world of the play allows for a certain ambiguity in the status of both their marriage and their children when seen from a fifth-century Athenian perspective,[39] the impact of this ambiguity is not to justify Jason's behaviour. It rather helps the audience to appreciate the nature of his motivation (for a higher-status union), and so intensifies the disquieting effect of the play. For if, as seems likely, Jason's patriarchal opinions chimed well with many in the audience, this increases the play's disruptive power, since his conduct is shown to have reprehensible results. Moreover, although Jason claims to be marrying for the sake of Medea and their children, his attempt to appear generous is undermined by his selfish style of expression: words for 'I', 'me', and 'my' occur with marked frequency throughout his speech (cf. 522, 526, 527, 531, 534, 535, 542, 544, 545, 547, 550, 566), creating the impression that Jason's real concern is his own comfort and prosperity.

Just as Jason denies that erotic desire played any part in his decision to marry Creon's daughter (cf. 556, 623), so he attributes this 'feminine' weakness to Medea, claiming that she would be able to accept his new marriage were it not for sexual jealousy (569-75):

> But you women are so far gone that if things in bed are going well, you think that you have everything; but if some misfortune occurs there, you regard the best and finest

things utterly hostile. Mortals should produce children from some other source and the female sex should not exist. Then there would be no evil for mankind.

The fantasy of a world without women is a staple of Greek misogyny.[40] No less stereotypical is the way Jason reduces Medea's anger to sexual dissatisfaction, for it is a *topos* of Greek thought to see women as obsessed with sex, while the female body is figured in both popular and medical thought as crucially susceptible to sexual desires and dysfunctions.[41] Yet the wider context of the play refutes Jason's crude interpretation of Medea's motives by showing that his narrow definition of the 'bed' as 'sex' (cf. 568, 570-1) is wholly inadequate. For Medea views the 'bed' as a symbol of the ties of marriage and women's wider domestic authority (cf. 265-6), not merely as a place of sexual fulfilment. Whereas Jason sees Medea as simply jealous and frustrated, the audience know that she is in fact provoked by his broken oath and betrayal of trust.

Significantly, the Chorus respond to the debate by strongly condemning Jason's conduct: 'in betraying your wife you are not acting justly' (578). Moreover, Medea herself adds an argument which completely undermines Jason's claim to have been acting in the best interests of his *philoi* (586-7): 'If you were not a coward, you should have persuaded me before making this marriage instead of keeping it a secret from your friends.' A husband could not secretly divorce his wife, but would usually expel her from his house. Jason, however, has simply taken a new wife behind Medea's back and he has allowed Creon to expel her from the country. Unable to grasp Medea's sense of hurt and betrayal, Jason repeats his insensitive offer of money (612-13). When Medea refuses it, he invokes the gods to witness his readiness to help (619-20). As in the rest of the scene, we see Jason absolutely unwilling to admit his share of responsibility for Medea's condition.

In their second stasimon, which comes immediately after Jason's exit, the Chorus speak from the perspective of married women, praying that men who fail to honour their *philoi* may die.[42] Their song thus accentuates the contrast between Jason's ingratitude and the conduct of the entering Aegeus, who agrees to protect Medea in return for her help in getting children. Aegeus' marked concern about his childlessness highlights the callous behaviour of Jason towards his own sons. Moreover, it is clear that Aegeus strongly disapproves of the wrong done to Medea personally, when he asks (695; cf. 703, 707): 'Has he really dared this most shameful deed?' After Aegeus has sworn to offer Medea refuge in Athens, the way is open for her revenge. With gruesome irony, Medea prepares to kill Jason's new bride with poisoned wedding gifts (784-9). In contrast to Deianeira in *The Women of Trachis*, Medea does not use the drug-anointed robe to recapture her husband's affections, but to destroy his new wife and so his chance of royal children (804-6).[43]

Yet Medea goes even further, for in order to punish Jason she will extinguish his line completely by killing her own children (792-6). The dramatic force of her declaration is overwhelming: for in Greek terms a child-killing mother negates not only the most basic human bond, but the definition of womanhood itself (note the Chorus' incredulous reaction: 856-65). Nevertheless, although the audience's attitude to Medea's revenge is crucially altered by her new plan, Medea's intense love for her children and her awareness of the enormity of her crime (cf. 795-6 'the murder of my dearest sons ... a most unholy deed') prevent her from being viewed as sub-human or bestial (cf. Chapter 4). That is, her action complicates the audience's moral response; it does not simply reassert male stereotypes of women. For the audience are led to appreciate the cost to Medea: by devastating Jason's *oikos*, she intends to punish *his* betrayal of it, yet this also means destroying those who are dearest to *her*. The conflict between Medea's heroic self-conception and her grief as a mother (cf. 807-10, 818) makes her decision both harrowing and awesome.

As Medea prepares to summon Jason, she instructs the Nurse to reveal nothing of her new plans, 'if you were born a woman' (823). The Nurse obeys, but the Chorus, though bound by a similar pledge of silence (cf. 259-67), plead with Medea not to kill her children (850-5). For them such an act breaks all bonds of female solidarity, but they are powerless to prevent it. Medea's second meeting with Jason is devised by her as a mirror-image of the first, with the crucial difference that Medea is here projecting a false picture of herself: where before she had spoken her mind and exposed Jason's cowardice, selfishness, and betrayal of his *philoi* (465-519), she now pretends to accept his position and plays the part of the submissive wife.

The scene is notable for Medea's skilful manipulation of gender stereotypes: she calls herself 'passionate' (870), 'foolish' (885), 'childish', and apologises for her 'female' tears (928). In a sense Medea's reinvention as a dutiful wife calls attention to the 'performance' of gender itself, but rather than concentrate too much on the meta-theatrical aspects (Medea is really a male actor in an ankle-length sleeved dress, etc.), which an Athenian audience would have perceived as the norm,[44] we should consider the power of Medea's behaviour to challenge male-generated stereotypes. For although Medea makes remarks that are critical of her sex (cf. 265-6, 384-5, 407-9), her use of them to deceive Jason (cf. 889-91) does not merely confirm conventional ideas of female deception, since the audience is encouraged to reject his deluded and patronising viewpoint (cf. 908-13, 944-5).

As the children depart with the gifts for Creon's daughter, Jason urges Medea to keep the precious objects for herself, confident that his new wife 'will put me before money' (963). There is an unconscious irony here, since Jason has put his own ambition for royal wealth and status before his obligation to his family. But with the news that Jason's bride has accepted the gifts (1003-4), Medea's revenge is under way and now she must decide whether to kill her own children. As she herself recognises, life without them will be 'full of pain and grief' (1036-7) and her long ordeal of indecision shows how desperate she is not to lose them. It has been argued that because Medea experiences regret and uncertainty, 'Euripides is, as it were, now subverting his own subversion'.[45] Yet Medea's hesitation and vulnerability do not undo her challenge to conventional gender ideology. On the contrary, her love for her children accentuates the conflict with her heroic desire for revenge, which in turn magnifies the tragic power of the scene.

In response to Medea's decision, the Chorus reflect (in chanted anapaests) on the anxieties and misfortunes of those who have children (1081-115). In contrast to their first stasimon (cf. 424-8), they now claim that there *are* female poets, even if only a few (1085-9). However, their positive change of mind on the possibility of female poetry is overshadowed by their opening remarks on the 'unfeminine' nature of their reflections (1081-4): 'Often before now I have gone through subtler discourses and entered upon greater arguments than the female sex should pursue.' The Chorus have abandoned their earlier confidence in the powers of female intelligence and it seems natural to connect this to Medea's declaration of infanticide. Her crime draws closer when the Messenger arrives to report the death of Creon's daughter. As the Chorus had predicted, Jason's new wife is now 'dressed as a bride among the dead' (985). For all her vanity (cf. 1156-66), the girl's destruction is horrific and leads to the death of her father.[46] The scene is thus set for the final element of Jason's punishment, the killing of his sons.

Significantly, although the Chorus regard Jason's suffering as just (1231-2),[47] the murder of the children (heard from inside the house) prompts them to lament the troubles brought upon

mankind by 'the bed of women' (1290-2). Yet while this continues the Chorus' criticism of the female sex seen in 1081-4 above,
the effect is not simply to reassert a patriarchal view of women,
for the play has shown how much Jason himself is to blame for
Medea's angry reaction to her slighted 'bed'. While Jason remains incapable of seeing anything more than purely sexual
jealousy in Medea's response (cf. 1367-9), the audience, who
have witnessed Medea's humiliation in the *oikos*, her only
significant area of authority, are encouraged to see beyond
Jason's stereotypical view and to appreciate the straitened
circumstances of women's lives.[48]

Medea's ambivalent status in the final scene as both betrayed, mourning mother and child-killing avenger means that
the play can be interpreted in very different ways. Where some
in the audience might view her as challenging negative stereotypes of women, others might see merely confirmation of their
worst suspicions. Thus one scholar claims that while Medea
exposes women's oppression and shows their intelligence, '[her]
overly literal imitation of an aristocratic masculine code, her
dehumanization, and her betrayal of her own sex could be said
equally to confirm women's ultimate incapacity for independence and civilized behavior'.[49] Similarly, another scholar
claims that Medea's escape 'supports the continued control of
actual women because it makes Medea's very freedom terrify-
ing'.[50] Yet this cannot be the whole story, for the audience are led
not only to see the justice of Medea's complaints, but also to
imagine the pressures which could drive a woman to kill her
own children. Amid the variety of possible responses to Medea's
actions, the sympathy created for her will have encouraged at
least some spectators (both male and female) to reassess their
preconceived notions of female autonomy and authority. The
play thus stands as one of the most radical and powerful
challenges to the dominant conceptions of gender in fifth-century
Athens (and beyond).

3

Greeks and Others

Medea comes from Colchis on the eastern shore of the Black Sea. Though parts of the coast of Colchis were settled by Greek colonisers in the sixth century BC, it remained in the fifth-century imagination a place far beyond the frontiers of Greek civilisation (barbarians being by definition 'uncivilised'). Medea's foreignness is raised as an issue from the very start of the play, and it is fundamental not only to how she is treated at Corinth (especially by Jason), but also to how the original Greek (and predominantly Athenian) audience viewed her reaction. Among the various versions of Medea's story, her foreignness and status as an outsider remain constant features of her experience and predicament. As we shall see, Euripides frequently explores the nature of Greek identity and often exposes the ethnic ideology that underlies the polarity of Greek and barbarian. *Medea* explores this ideology by presenting Medea as both a quintessentially dangerous barbarian and as a recognisably 'Greek' wife and mother. By presenting these contradictory qualities in the same person, Euripides encourages his Panhellenic audience to question the validity of the Greek / barbarian opposition itself.[1] Unfortunately, the play's challenging impact in this important political realm has often been downplayed or altogether overlooked: Denys Page notoriously commented on Medea's actions, 'Because she was a foreigner she could kill her children; because she was a witch she could escape in a chariot.'[2] Yet such an approach mistakenly defuses the play's interrogatory power and risks reducing it to a document of crude ethnic chauvinism.

The role played by literature and myth in Greek and Athenian self-definition has been a major theme of much recent work on Greek tragedy.[3] Though one should take care not to exaggerate the primitive 'us and them' mentality behind such self-definition, there was a more or less widely accepted distinction between Greeks and non-Greeks, and a more or less widely accepted assumption of the superiority of the former.[4] Nevertheless, such distinctions and assumptions co-existed with extensive borrowing from non-Greek cultures.[5] Furthermore, such cultural borrowing was especially characteristic of cosmopolitan Athens, so much so that the Old Oligarch could criticise Athenian multiculturalism from a conservative viewpoint, condemning the Athenians' combination of Greek and barbarian elements in their dialect, lifestyle, and dress.[6] But while such a hardline dichotomy of Greek and barbarian (and even Athenian and non-Athenian)[7] was being espoused and supported by some Athenians,[8] we also hear voices raised against the monochrome anti-barbarian view, especially in the surviving works of the Sophists, the histories of Herodotus and Thucydides, and the plays of Euripides.[9] We should therefore see their reflections on Greek and non-Greek as a response to a pressing issue, particularly in Athens, where tensions resulting from immigration and ethnic difference will have been most pronounced.

Before we look at how *Medea* powerfully deconstructs the ideology and rhetoric of Greek superiority, it is important that we consider how the basic dichotomy of Greek and barbarian came about. Centres of Panhellenic festival and cult developed in the Archaic period at Delphi, Olympia, Isthmia, and Nemea. These popular and prestigious events point to a burgeoning sense of Greekness, since they celebrated the participants' common heritage as Hellenes rather than their local loyalties as, for example, Athenians, Thebans, or Syracusans (even if victories in the Panhellenic games could subsequently be used to bolster power and prestige at a local level). The late Archaic and early Classical periods also saw the systematisation of Greek myth,[10] as various figures (including the author of the Hesiodic *Catalogue of Women*, Hecataeus of Miletus, Pherecydes of Athens, and Hellanicus of Lesbos) constructed intricate and interlocking genealogies based on the myths and thereby fostered a sense of a shared Greek past and common identity.[11] But although there are a few instances of anti-barbarian sentiment in Archaic literature,[12] a major shift in attitudes to non-Greeks is evident after the Persian invasions of 490 and 480-79 BC: 'The full development of both conceptions [Greek and barbarian] and their combination into the great antithesis was brought about by the clash with Persia, the arch-enemy of Greece and the destroyer of Greek culture.'[13] The Persian attempt to subjugate Greece and their defeat by a smaller state solidified the notion of Greek superiority,[14] an assumption that extended beyond military and tactical prowess[15] to cover the full range of social, political, and cultural practices.[16]

At the first performance of *Medea* in 431 BC were many people whose parents and grandparents had been driven from their homes by the Persians. They had seen their temples and property destroyed, and such violence will have bred an extreme suspicion of all things eastern and non-Greek which would be passed on from one generation to the next. It is all the more remarkable, therefore, that Euripides should repeatedly challenge the polarity of Greek and barbarian in his plays. He does so with especial force in *Medea* by having Jason choose to foreground his wife's foreign origins in the hope that this will draw attention away from his own unscrupulous conduct. Interestingly, Pindar (*Pythian* 4.212) describes the Colchians as dark-faced, while Herodotus (2.104) describes them as dark-skinned and woolly-haired, yet there is no indication in the text of Euripides' play that Medea wore a black mask. (Whether she wore a barbarian costume in the final scene will be considered below.) Nevertheless, her status (or rather, lack of status) as a barbarian is a crucial aspect of her experience and an important factor in the audience's response to the play.

By presenting Jason too as an outsider in Corinth, the play explores the pressures facing him, a proud but powerless aristocrat from a separate Greek kingdom. And by depicting Jason's attempt to better his status, the play also stresses the crucial difference between him and Medea: as a Greek, Jason can do something to improve his lot, whereas Medea, once she has been abandoned by him, cannot, but must rely on charity. Moreover, Medea's powerlessness as a barbarian is compounded by her status as a woman: the categories of female and foreigner both stand in opposition to the dominant agenda of the Greek male (represented here by the dynastic agreement made between Creon and Jason).[17] Medea is thus doubly disadvantaged, first as a woman, powerless to prevent Jason's new marriage, and secondly as a foreigner, who is automatically suspected of violence, deceit, and lawlessness. Yet just as the play provokes the audience to think about the injustices done to one excluded group (women), so it exposes the prejudice faced by another (foreigners).

The play begins by presenting Medea's predicament from the viewpoint of her old Nurse, a fellow Colchian, who laments their contact with the Greek Argonauts (1-2): 'If only the *Argo*'s hull had never flown to the land of Colchis through the dark-blue Clashing Rocks.' The Clashing Rocks (or Symplegades), situated at the Bosphorus (the narrow channel at the entrance to the Black Sea), mark a dangerous boundary-point between the Greek and non-Greek worlds. Significantly, however, since the speaker is a Colchian, the origins of the present trouble are first seen from the 'other side', as it were, and it is the incursion of Greeks which is regretted. Their arrival not only afflicted the Nurse's mistress with irrational passion (8), but also led Medea to kill Jason's uncle, Pelias, by tricking his daughters (9-10). And yet, the Nurse emphasises, despite these unfortunate beginnings, Medea has succeeded in ingratiating herself with the Corinthians (11-12).[18]

As well as pleasing her host community, Medea has complied with Jason in every respect (13), as a wife should (14-15).[19] Thus, though a barbarian (and a slave), the Nurse voices the conventional Greek view of a woman's role. Her remark short-circuits the stereotype of the lustful barbarian (cf. *Andromache* 240-4), and this reversal is reflected in the conduct of Jason and Medea, since Medea remains faithful to her husband, while Jason abandons his wife for a younger woman. (Though Jason later denies that desire played any part in his decision (556, 593), the Chorus' reflections on desire and its consequences (627-62) apply to his situation as well.) Jason's treatment of Medea has brought dishonour upon her, and this prompts the Nurse to reflect on the dangers of leaving one's homeland (34-5), since the absence of *philoi* (relatives and friends) means that one is always at risk of being abused. The Nurse's words encourage us to see Jason as a selfish coward, exploiting Medea's weakness and vulnerability as a foreigner (and a woman) in Greek society (cf. 435-8).[20]

This critical picture of Jason is developed further in the meeting between the Nurse and the Paidagogos. The Paidagogos reports a rumour that Creon intends to banish Medea and her children from Corinth (70-3); Jason, however, is doing nothing to prevent this (74-7). Having focused on Medea's dishonour in her opening speech, the Nurse now addresses the children directly and stresses their father's disloyalty (82-4):

O children, do you hear what kind of a man your father is towards you? May he not die – for he's my master – but he stands convicted of treating his loved ones badly.

For Jason to damage his sons' interests in this way, in addition to dishonouring his wife, is deeply reprehensible, and the condemnation of his behaviour by the household slaves is echoed not only by Medea herself, but also by the Chorus of Corinthian Women. Significantly, these Greeks openly express their sympathy for the 'unhappy Colchian woman' (132). Moreover, they describe Medea's household as 'joined [literally "mixed", *kekratai*] with me in friendship' (cf. 179, 181). We are again reminded of Medea's success in adapting to her new Greek environment. The Chorus' concern for Medea is also a foil to the specious concern of Jason: unlike her own husband, they care about Medea's distress and do not make an issue of her nationality.

When we hear Medea's voice from inside the house, her cries move from stark prayers for self-destruction (96-7, 144-7) to a more elaborate attack on Jason's faithlessness (160-3):

> O mighty Themis and lady Artemis, do you see what I suffer, though I bound my accursed husband with mighty oaths?

Jason's broken promise to Medea is one of the major leitmotifs of the play. When the Nurse has outlined the breakdown of her mistress' marriage, the first we hear of Medea's reaction is that she is invoking Jason's oaths and calling upon the gods to witness his treachery (21-3). The Chorus immediately take up Medea's grievance and describe her passage from Colchis to Greece in terms that strikingly emphasise the importance of Jason's promises (208-12):

> Having suffered unjustly, she invokes Themis, daughter of Zeus, goddess of oaths, who brought her to Greece across the sea, through the dark waters to the salty gateway of the boundless Black Sea.

Themis, guardian of oaths, is pictured as bringing Medea through the Bosphorus to Greece. The description reminds us that there was more to Medea's decision to leave her native land than mere irrational passion: she also went relying on Jason's fidelity and honesty. He was not only bound to Medea by a formal oath, but also indebted to her for accepting his supplication and so ensuring the success of his mission to Colchis (cf. 492-8), yet these powerful obligations have counted for nothing. The Chorus express the shock and disgrace of this breach of trust in their first stasimon: 'The grace of oaths has departed, and shame remains no longer in the great expanse of Greece, but has flown to the skies' (439-40). Since the Greeks liked to think that they were trustworthy, while barbarians were not,[21] Jason's behaviour overturns the stereotype of barbarian perfidy, especially when contrasted with Medea's loyalty to him. Significantly, when Medea later announces her plan to kill her own children, she stresses Jason's lies ('persuaded by the words of a Greek', 801-2). The audience is frequently reminded that it is the Greek Jason who has broken his word and abandoned his family, and as a result any wholly positive Greek self-perception is undermined.

In her opening speech Medea herself draws attention to her status as an outsider, remarking that 'a foreigner in particular must comply with the city's ways' (222). Since her words must be seen as part of her overall rhetorical strategy to win the Chorus' support, the fact that Medea chooses to foreground her own foreignness is significant and shows how confident she is that she has adapted to her new society and earned thereby the Corinthians' approval. Although Medea's main appeal to the Chorus is as a fellow woman, eliding the ethnic divide (230-51), she does use her isolation and helplessness in a foreign land to stir their sympathy (255-8). Importantly, the Chorus support Medea as they would any other Greek woman (267-8) and, in contrast to Medea's disaffection from Jason, their eventual estrangement from her is never framed in ethnic terms.

When Creon comes to announce his decree of banishment, the first reason that he gives is his fear of Medea's skills in drugs and magic: 'You are clever and have knowledge of many evil arts' (285). Interestingly, Jason himself is connected to drugs (and especially to their healing power as medicines) in early Greek myth (*Iason* can mean 'he who heals'). However, as C.J. Mackie notes, Jason's knowledge of drugs and magic has been transferred to Medea as part of the myth's articulation of fundamental ethnic (and gender) differences: 'It is one thing for a Greek hero to employ such dangerous practices, but quite another for a foreign woman to do so. Jason's lack of knowledge of drugs in the literature, and Medea's extensive use of them, are different sides of the same coin. Both of them in their own ways help to reinforce notions of self-identity and difference, between Greeks and barbarians on the one hand, and men and women on the other.'[22] Both Creon and Jason, powerful Greek males, construct their enemy Medea as a clever, and therefore potentially dangerous, female. Yet while Medea's 'cleverness' is perceived by Creon as sinister (285), its more positive aspects are brought out in the scene with Aegeus (677, 716-18; cf. 11-12). Moreover, we should take care not to exaggerate Medea's magical side in the play: she certainly has an acute knowledge of drugs (for both good and evil ends),[23] but until her miraculous escape in the Chariot of the Sun her supernatural aspects are not stressed.[24] Were Medea presented from the start as anything other than a recognisably human figure, the play would be very different and far less powerful.

 While her opponents perceive Medea as a threatening barbarian presence, Medea's own conception of herself is essentially heroic and strikingly 'Greek'.[25] Like the most status-sensitive of Greek heroes, Medea is determined to avoid the laughter of her enemies (cf. 383, 404, 797, 1049-50, 1355, 1362).

Thus, as a foreign woman behaving like a Greek man, Medea's heroic self-conception cuts across the polarities of both gender and ethnicity. Though Medea's 'heroism' will turn out to have horrendous consequences, her resolution, pride, and clarity of purpose are admirable, and they contrast strongly with Jason's evasions and self-deception. Jason's own patronising air of (ethnic) superiority is clear from his first 'defence speech' (522-75), where he claims that by introducing Medea to the benefits of Greek civilisation he has more than repaid her past services to him. Jason contrasts the violence of barbarian society with the lawful existence of the Greeks (536-8). Barbarian lawlessness was a staple of Greek ethnic discourse (e.g. *Andromache* 168-76), while the rule of law was seen as a peculiarly Greek achievement (cf. Herodotus 7.104, Thucydides 2.37). Yet Jason's rhetoric of Greek justice is undermined by his own devious and selfish conduct. Similarly, it is the barbarian Medea, not Jason, who shows concern for the bonds of *philia*, and this too reverses the stereotype (cf. *Hecuba* 328-9). Finally, Jason's argument that being brought to Greece has benefited Medea 'elides the point that Medea has reiterated: that she came to Greece *as Jason's wife*, and for no other reason'.[26]

It is significant that Jason is alone in exploiting Medea's foreignness; neither Creon nor the Chorus ever use her ethnicity against her. This is not merely a mark of Jason's moral and intellectual shallowness, but also a sign of the weakness of his case. Medea has every right to feel aggrieved at Jason's deception, and his verbal appeals to Greek superiority and justice cannot disguise this (cf. 580-5). Nevertheless, insofar as Jason seeks to justify his decision to remarry on the grounds that this will help his and Medea's sons (559-68), there are features of his situation which would incline an Athenian male to be sympathetic. For after Pericles' citizenship law of 451/50 BC a 'foreign' (i.e. non-Athenian) wife became a liability, since offspring of such a marriage were banned from the descent group which now made up the exclusive club of Athenian citizens. If the undesirability of a foreign wife in Athens is here projected back into mythical Corinth, an Athenian audience might have more understanding for Jason's position and his concern for his sons' future prospects.[27] However, while the audience are led to appreciate Jason's alleged motives, they are also led to criticise his actual conduct, for it becomes clear that his primary goal is his own royal power, not the welfare of his sons, whose exile he accepts (cf. 74-7). Medea demolishes Jason's rhetoric of generosity and family concern, pointing out that he acted in total secrecy from his family (585-7), and she also pinpoints the real motive behind his desire for a new wife: his fear that marriage to a foreigner would become a source of disgrace (591-2). Medea's insight into her conventional husband's embarrassment is acute and undermines his claims to be acting purely for the safety of Medea and their children.

Jason's attempt to present Medea as a benighted and lawless barbarian is further undercut by the appearance of Aegeus, king of Athens, who greets Medea as an old friend (663-4). Though the audience were probably familiar with stories of Medea's later activities in Athens (cf. Chapter 1), Euripides seems to be innovating here in having Aegeus turn up in Corinth, where his appearance comes as a surprise, albeit a welcome one for Medea. As Grube points out, the Aegeus scene 'gives us a glimpse of Medea as she was before the disaster ... it reminds us that the deserted Colchian mistress was a princess in her own right who could meet kings on equal terms; it also gives us the first unprejudiced view of Jason's conduct, and this is anything but favourable (690-707)'.[28] In fact, Aegeus considers Jason's behaviour 'most shameful' (695) and his response guides that of the Athenian audience. Unlike Jason, Aegeus reacts according to whether acts are right or wrong, not whether the agents are Greek or barbarian. The picture of Athens as a place that welcomes innocent refugees is flattering,[29] but Medea's reception there is complicated not only by her imminent revenge at Corinth, but also by her future actions in Athens itself.[30]

The (Athenian) audience is encouraged to reflect on the significance of Aegeus' agreement by the choral song that follows his departure (824-65). In the first strophic pair the Corinthian Chorus depict an Athens that is secure, cultured, and blessed by the gods (824-45).[31] Yet this peaceful vision is shattered by the imagined arrival and acceptance of a child-killer (846-50). In other words, the Chorus hope to dissuade Medea from her new plan of revenge by urging her to consider her impact upon (an idealised) Athens.[32] And their question 'How can Athens accept a child-murderer?' is also directed to the audience, prompting them to reconsider their city's hallowed past. The song is thus more complex than it may appear: there is certainly praise of Athens,[33] but the city is also seen as the potential refuge of a child-killer, which is disturbing, and Medea's reception brings home to the audience the fragility of their city's well-being.[34] Nevertheless, the revelation of Medea's infanticide does not merely reinscribe the old prejudices of the lawless barbarian, since she remains in many respects a sympathetic and admirable figure, especially as she struggles *against* herself to perfect her revenge (cf. Chapter 4). As we shall see, even Medea's problematic future in Athens does not mean that the audience automatically share Jason's response in the final scene.

In line with his earlier rhetoric of barbarian violence (536-8), Jason interprets Medea's actions as proof of his polarised worldview (1329-32):

May you die! I can think straight now, but I was insane before when I brought you from your house in a barbarian land to a Greek home, great evil that you are, who betrayed your father and the country that nurtured you.

Jason's shameless evasion of responsibility (Medea is a 'traitor', while his own liability is denied) encourages the audience to question the simple contrast between civilised Greece and barbarian Colchis. Jason's hypocrisy is further underlined by his claim that 'There is no Greek woman who would have brought herself to do such a thing' (1339-40). Yet the Chorus have just mentioned one Greek woman, Ino (1283-5), who killed her own children, and Greek myth told of others (e.g. Agave, Procne, Althaea).[35] Thus both the dramatic situation and the audience's knowledge of myth direct them to challenge the simplistic conclusion that 'Jason himself understood the truth in the end'.[36]

The play's exploration of barbarian stereotypes will have been all the more vivid if Medea wore exotic foreign costume throughout.[37] Here, in the final scene, Medea's status (and visual impact) as outsider is both ramified and complicated by her *deus*-like appearance in the Chariot of the Sun. For Medea predicts that she will now escape to Athens 'to live with Aegeus' (1385),[38] potentially triggering the audience's awareness of her dangerous future there. Yet even if the audience were unaware of Medea's attack on Aegeus' son, Theseus,[39] the incorporation of a child-killer within their royal family is disturbing. Nevertheless, neither the shock of Medea's terrible revenge nor her departure for Athens can annul the audience's experience of her suffering. For in the course of the play they have been brought to understand that Medea herself is not solely to blame for her ruin and that Jason's rhetoric of Greek superiority is merely an excuse for his own treachery. Indeed, in their final passage of dialogue Medea re-emphasises Jason's faithlessness and implies that the gods condemn his conduct as well (1391-2): 'Which god or divine power listens to you, an oath-breaker and deceiver of foreign guests?'

Looking beyond *Medea*, we can see that many of Euripides' surviving works explore the polarity of Greek and barbarian.[40]

By presenting both virtuous barbarians (e.g. *Andromache* 243-4, *Hecuba* 577-80, *Trojan Women* 667-8, *Helen* 47) and 'barbaric' Greeks (*Trojan Women* 764-5, *Iphigenia in Tauris* 1174), his plays show that the popular distinction between Greek (good) and non-Greek (bad) soon breaks down. And by turning Greek claims to superiority on their head, Euripides is doing more than producing 'striking rhetorical effects':[41] his plays challenge the prevailing ethnic ideology of their time.[42] In the case of *Medea*, Jason's conduct cannot be justified simply by saying that Medea is a foreigner. For Euripides leads the audience to feel sympathy for her vulnerability and presents her reaction in typically Greek heroic terms. To be sure, some may have regarded the infanticide as merely confirming their prejudices and their superior Greek identity, but the play as a whole encourages a more nuanced response, which sees the cracks in Jason's (and their own society's) rhetoric of difference and inferiority.

4

Medea's Revenge

Medea's determination upon revenge lies at the heart of the play, driving the plot towards its horrific climax.[1] It is a striking feature of Greek tragedy that so many of the surviving plays involve acts of retribution; this is closely linked to the prevalence of vengeance as a story-pattern in Greek myth, which in turn is connected to the importance of honour and revenge in ancient Greek society. For in a community where concern for one's *timê* ('honour') was paramount, injury to one's *timê* demanded a retaliatory response from the victim. Moreover, this obsessive concern with honour was accompanied by a no less fundamental ethic of reciprocity, which dictated that one do good to one's friends (*philoi*) and harm to one's enemies (*echthroi*).[2] As both husband and former suppliant of Medea, Jason is bound to her by the closest ties of friendship (*philia*). Yet by arranging his new marriage without regard to the welfare of either Medea or their children, Jason has reversed the principle of 'helping friends and harming enemies', treating his closest *philoi* as if they were *echthroi* and abandoning his responsibilities towards them. Moreover, Medea has helped Jason greatly, not only saving his life and his mission to Colchis, but also bearing him male heirs (cf. 476-82, 488-91), so that his betrayal of his closest *philoi* is particularly unjust and painful.

Medea responds to Jason's injustice with a typically heroic desire to see her enemies punished and her injury avenged.[3] Yet her heroic response is complicated by her gender, for women were not expected to show, or act upon, such a 'male' desire for retaliation. Euripides depicts female victims turned avengers in a number of plays (cf. *The Children of Heracles, Hecuba*), and like Phaedra (*Hippolytus*), Electra (*Electra*), and (unwittingly) Creusa (*Ion*), Medea directs her revenge against a member of her own family. Yet Medea's heroic persona is far more fully developed than that of any other female avenger, and her revenge is all the more shocking for being consciously channelled through her own children. In this respect *Medea* is an unusual and uniquely harrowing tragedy of revenge, since it presents an act of violent retribution that is simultaneously an act of self-destruction. For rather than killing Jason (a *philos* turned *echthros*) Medea kills her dearest *philoi*, her own children. In ancient Greek society (as in our own) infanticide was viewed as a peculiarly evil and abnormal act, almost an effacement of human nature. Yet, because Medea's fury is concentrated within the female domain of the family, this is precisely what her revenge ethic leads her to do.

Medea's passionate nature and her fearful temper are repeatedly evoked by both the Nurse and the Chorus in the play's opening scene (cf. 44-5, 98-9, 142-3, 176-7).[4] We learn that Medea may pose a threat to her own children if her anger is not assuaged (36-7, 90-5, 101-4, 117-18, 181-3), and Medea herself calls for the children's destruction from inside the house (112-14): 'Accursed children of a hateful mother, may you die with your father, and the whole house fall in ruins!' She also prays for the death of Jason's bride and the collapse of the royal palace (163-4). Thus the opening scene creates suspense and foreboding over the identity of Medea's victims (cf. 108-10), while raising the terrible possibility that her innocent children may suffer undeservedly for their father's wrongdoing (116-17). Adding to the threatening atmosphere, Medea reacts to her disgrace by wishing she herself were dead (96-7, 151-2, 227). Yet, as soon as she appears on stage and recounts her sufferings to the Chorus, we see that Medea's wish for self-destruction is dwarfed by her desire to punish her enemies. And there are already signs that Medea's sense of personal dishonour is matched by public, religious condemnation of Jason's conduct, for as well as abandoning his family, he has broken his solemn and divine oath of loyalty to Medea (160-3, 208-13).

In her first encounter with the Chorus the details of Medea's revenge are still unformed, yet she asks them for their support (in the form of secrecy) should she discover some way to punish Jason (259-63). By appealing to their shared misfortune as wives and mothers (230-51), Medea aligns the Chorus of Corinthian women against her husband, the 'vilest of men' (229), whose punishment the Chorus consider justified (267). Significantly, Medea speaks only of harming Jason, not of harming Jason's new wife or the royal family, making it easier for the Chorus to comply with her plan. Medea's defiant speech to them after Creon's departure represents the most striking confirmation thus far of her heroic self-conception. As she counters their attitude of hopelessness ('Some god has cast you, Medea, into an overwhelming sea of troubles', 362-3), Medea's emphasis on the necessary and immediate punishment of her enemies forcefully displays her heroic pride and resolution: '[This day] I shall make corpses of three of my enemies, the father, the daughter, and my husband' (374-5; cf. 367-8). A further typically heroic aspect of Medea's motivation is her obsessive concern with the ridicule of her enemies; hence her fear that she may get caught while performing her revenge and be killed herself, providing her enemies with a chance to laugh at her (381-3; cf. 398, 404). In Greek eyes few things were more shameful than when one's enemies rejoiced over one's misfortune, and heroic figures exhibit an exceptionally intense sensitivity to such mockery. In her speech Medea presents this feeling of *Schadenfreude* from both sides, as it were, for as well as her fear of her enemies' laughter she also expresses her own pleasure at their imagined death, as she appraises the various methods she might use to kill them (fire, sword, or poison, 376-85).

Though Medea envisions using the heroic 'male' weapon, the sword, and sacrificing her own life in the act of revenge (393-4), she states a clear preference for poison: 'Best is the direct route, in which I am particularly skilled, and kill them with poison' (384-5). Significantly, Medea uses a first person plural verb here and so her words may also be interpreted as 'in which we [i.e. women] are particularly skilled': the guile and secrecy of poison meant that it was figured in (male-generated) Greek thought as a peculiarly 'female' weapon, and Medea's explicitly cunning (and 'feminine') approach creates a powerful clash with her 'male' ethos of heroic self-assertion. Nevertheless, the play is far from being a simple attack on women's stealth and destructiveness. For Medea's reaction to her dishonour is ultimately directed against her own children, and her violence, which she herself abhors, represents not only a perversion of the code of 'helping friends and harming enemies', but also a critique of women's constrained existence and exploitation.

As the Chorus observe in their first stasimon, Jason's treachery has reduced Medea to the status of an 'exile without rights' (438), and in the following scene, their first on-stage meeting, Medea gives full vent to her anger and sense of injustice. The terms in which she sums up Jason's conduct reveal her own values of loyalty and reciprocity: 'This is not boldness or courage, to do harm to one's friends and then look them in the face, but the worst of all human sicknesses, shamelessness!' (469-72). Lack of *aidôs* ('shame', 'respect') counted as one of the greatest moral failings among the Greeks, and Medea perceives Jason's presence before her, despite his betrayal of his pledge, as a particularly shocking example of it. She outlines her hopeless and undeserved situation to Jason as if he were her 'friend', since this will reveal his shameful behaviour still further (499-501). As Medea explains, it was for Jason's sake that she

84

betrayed and abandoned her own *philoi* in Colchis and killed *his* enemy Pelias (502-8). In other words, though she sacrificed her own ties of *philia* to help him, he has paid her back ('in return for these things', 510) by abandoning her.

Insensitive to her isolation and estrangement, Jason attempts to present his new marriage as a benefit to both Medea and their children (548-50). He cannot, however, properly answer Medea's charge that he went behind her back and married *secretly* (586-7), and this explodes his claim to have been acting in the best interests of his family. In fact, Jason is only interested in securing an easy life for himself, and to achieve this he has shown himself willing to put expediency (a secret marriage) before justice (openness to his friends).[5] In response to Jason's shabby rhetoric, and with an ominous forecast of her revenge, Medea states her opinion that 'the unjust man who is clever with words incurs *the greatest punishment*' (580-1), which well describes the kind of 'living death' (cf. 1310, 1326) she will inflict upon Jason. Though he may now enjoy good fortune, while she goes 'friendless into exile' (604, a description that prepares for the Aegeus scene to come), Medea ends their confrontation on a threatening note (625-6): 'For perhaps – and the gods will agree – you will make such a marriage as will bring you tears.'

It is important to our understanding and evaluation of Medea's revenge that we see it gradually forming in response to the words and actions not only of her 'enemies', Creon and Jason, but also of her 'friend', Aegeus. As Medea's *philos* (cf. 664), Aegeus is appalled by Jason's treacherous behaviour: 'Jason wrongs me, though he suffered from me no harm' (692). It is also significant for Medea's response to her dishonour, and to the audience's sense of her *developing* revenge, that the scene between her and Aegeus should place so much emphasis on the miseries of childlessness (cf. 670, 714-22). Won over by Medea's promise of children, Aegeus is made to swear a great oath to protect her against her enemies (746-53), and his pledge not only draws attention to the sacrilege of Jason's earlier oath-breaking, but also creates a contrast between the two men, for while Aegeus' oath is intended to secure the birth of children, Jason's perjury will soon result in the death of his two sons. Moreover, Aegeus' oath is sealed with a prayer for the destruction of his own line (if he should impiously break his word, 754-5), which is exactly the kind of *divine* punishment that will soon be visited upon Jason by Medea.

Medea had earlier told the Chorus that, if a 'bastion of safety' should appear to her, she would 'go about this murder with guile and secrecy' (390-1). Thus, since Aegeus, who came as her friend (663-4), has now departed as her sworn protector (759-63), Medea can finally look forward to punishing her enemies.[6] The great speech in which she outlines the full extent of her plans (764-810) marks a major turning point in the play, for the revelation of infanticide radically alters the attitude of both the Chorus and the audience to Medea's revenge, undermining the Chorus' sympathy (cf. 773, 'Do not expect to receive my words with pleasure') and challenging the audience to confront (and make sense of) Medea's decision. As her opening invocation makes clear (764), Medea believes that she has justice (indeed, the goddess Justice herself) on her side, and she presents the murders to come as a 'glorious victory' over her enemies (765). Yet her insistent rhetoric of helping friends and harming enemies (cf. 767, 809-10) is exploded by the declaration 'I shall kill my own children' (792-3: here the crucial words 'my own' are delayed to first position in the new line, increasing their impact).

As we saw in Chapter 1, it is likely that Euripides innovated in making Medea deliberately responsible for the death of her children. Although there have been earlier hints of danger from their mother (cf. 36-7, 90-5, 100-4, 112-14), Medea's decision to kill the children with her own hand comes as a great shock to both Chorus and audience. The shock is compounded for the

4. Medea's Revenge

Athenian audience by the fact that Medea reveals her plan immediately after the Aegeus scene. As Aegeus left, Medea prayed to Zeus, Helios, and Justice, and the audience may have expected that Medea, a helpless and unjustly treated refugee, would soon be vindicated with Athens' help. As in other tragedies (e.g. Sophocles, *Oedipus at Colonus*, Euripides, *The Children of Heracles*, *Suppliant Women*, *Heracles*), Athens seems to be playing its familiar role of defender of the weak, but such an impression is suddenly and powerfully subverted by Medea's decision to kill her children, for Aegeus will now be forced either to break his divine oath or receive a polluted child-killer within Athens.

As she outlines her deception and punishment of Jason (774ff.), Medea begins with the murder of Creon's daughter, and the audience may have expected her to continue by detailing her earlier plan to kill her 'three enemies', Creon, his daughter, and Jason (cf. 374-5). However, rather than killing Jason and his new family, Medea devises a more painful punishment, allowing Jason to live, but making him witness the annihilation of not only his new *oikos* and its promise of descendants (cf. 794, 803-6), but also the offspring of his former *oikos*. In other words, the murder of Creon's daughter as well as Jason's children destroys his entire line (past, present, and future), a catastrophe which Jason himself will live to suffer.[7] Yet amid the collapse of Jason's life it is Medea's murder of their children which stands out as the most shocking and disturbing aspect of her revenge, and it is to this aspect of Jason's punishment alone that the Chorus object (811-13). For rather than the notional loss of possible future children, Medea's act involves the death of living children, and the horror is increased by the identity of the killer, their own mother. In ancient Greece (as in all human societies) there was a strong taboo against infanticide (despite the practice of exposure), and Medea's repudiation of the nurturing maternal role will have seemed especially horrendous.[8]

Medea's child-killing revenge is both a simple, directed act and one with paradoxical ramifications. It is clear-cut and directed insofar as it punishes Jason's betrayal of his marriage to Medea by destroying the most concrete embodiment of that union, their children.[9] Medea's choice of punishment brings home to Jason that he cannot shirk off responsibility to his *philoi* and expect to escape the consequences.[10] Yet her revenge is also paradoxical and problematic, for it is simultaneously an act of *self*-destruction and one which punishes Jason's betrayal of the bonds of *philia* by violating them in an even more appalling manner. Moreover, as Medea's agonised hesitation shows (1042ff.), she has chosen a form of revenge which is the most harrowingly painful for herself as well as her 'enemy'. Significantly, even as she announces the infanticide, presenting it as a way of defeating her enemies and quenching their laughter (cf. 797), Medea's language betrays both her reluctance to kill her sons (whom she calls 'most dear', 795) and her awareness of the act's impiety (she calls it a 'most unholy deed', 796).

The declaration of infanticide has a tremendous impact on the direction and impact of the play. The Chorus change from supporters to opponents of Medea's revenge and the audience is simultaneously challenged to reassess its sympathy for her. As the Chorus respond in song to Medea's horrific plan, they cannot believe that she will be able to perform such an unnatural act (856-65). Their anguished questions foreshadow Medea's agony in the following scene as she debates whether to go through with the murder or take her sons with her to Athens (1021ff.). But before Medea is confronted with this decision she must secure the first part of her revenge, begging Jason's forgiveness for her earlier 'foolishness' and 'childishness' (890-3), and arranging for the poisoned gifts to be sent to his new wife. Their encounter evokes conflicting responses, for although the audience may enjoy Medea's subtle manipulation of Jason's vanity, they cannot fail to be aware that his deception brings the infanticide closer to completion. When the children are brought out of the house (894ff.), the ironies of the scene become especially harsh and affecting: Medea bursts into tears (903, 922; cf. 861) and Jason fails to understand why she is so fearful of the children's future. While Jason pictures his sons growing up to be 'victorious over my enemies' (920-1), the audience know that they are being made instruments of his own destruction. Indeed, the children are tools of Medea's revenge twice over, since it is they who carry the fatal gifts to Jason's new wife (969-75). When the Chorus lament the children's departure, 'They are already on their way to death' (977), their word for death (*phonos*) can also mean 'murder' and evokes the killing of Creon's daughter as well as the infanticide.

Significantly, though the Chorus deplore the murder of the children, they express sympathy for Medea's grief and continue to criticise Jason's 'lawless' betrayal of his marriage (996-1001). The Chorus' attitude, torn between pity for Medea's loss and disgust at her crime, mirrors the conflicted response of the audience. The infanticide is clearly evil, but our response to Medea is not one of simple condemnation, for she herself acknowledges the wickedness of her act and struggles against it. Moreover, her internal struggle is presented in the most vivid and heart-rending terms, and with the children physically present beside her. Once the children have returned from their mission to Creon's daughter, Medea feels that their fate is sealed, and her silence puzzles the Paidagogos (1005): 'Why do you stand there devastated when things are going well for you?' When the Paidagogos then asks why she is weeping, Medea's reply is remarkable, for it reveals her own awareness that her mode of revenge is wrong: 'I must weep, old man. For the gods and I in my foolishness have devised it so' (1013-14). Yet Medea's mention of the gods also alerts us to the moral complexity of her actions: for although the infanticide seems (by human standards) cruel and unnatural, Medea never doubts that her revenge has divine support.

After the Paidagogos is ordered back inside the house (1019-20), Medea is left alone with the children and delivers her final words to them. Yet this is more than a simple speech of farewell: Medea is struck by doubts about her deed, creating one of the most famous and moving speeches in surviving tragedy, as she fluctuates between love for her sons and desire for revenge. The first part of her speech (1021-39) is addressed to the children themselves; here Medea laments a far more literal 'loss' of her sons than the Paidagogos had envisaged: whereas he imagined the children remaining behind in Corinth as Medea goes into exile, she sees them departing for Hades (cf. 1017-18, 1021-2, 1039, 1073). Suddenly, as she notices her sons' oblivious smiles (1040-1), Medea begins to hesitate (1042ff.), and she changes her mind several times in the course of the speech, first rejecting the murders (1042-8), then seeing such rejection as a mark of cowardice (1049-55), then urging herself to spare the children's lives (1056-8), and finally declaring their deaths to be necessary (1059ff.). Some scholars find these multiple changes of mind excessive, and lines 1056-80 (containing Medea's third and fourth volte-faces) have become one of the most controversial and frequently deleted passages in tragedy.[11] In his Oxford Classical Text (1984), J. Diggle considers the entire passage spurious,[12] while other scholars have defended less extensive deletions.[13] However, to assume that signs of 'incoherence' in Medea's speech must necessarily point to spuriousness is to fail to grasp the dramatic power of her internal debate.[14] For Medea's confusion and hesitation enhance her humanity and so increase our involvement in her predicament. Most importantly, Medea's monologue reveals her revenge to be truly pitiful and tragic, as we see her desire for retribution clashing with her feelings as a mother.

The structure and movement of Medea's debate are skilfully

shaped; the many questions, replies, and changes of direction express the speaker's psychological uncertainty and emotional disorder. Moved by the sight of her children, Medea first rejects her plans and pinpoints the excruciating paradox at the heart of her revenge (1046-7): 'Why should I cause their father pain through their suffering, when doing so will win twice as much suffering for myself?' But Medea's heroic fear of letting her enemies go unpunished reasserts itself (1049-50) and she orders the children inside the house,[15] bidding those who should not attend their 'sacrifice' to stay away (1053-5). At a normal sacrifice it was customary to bid unsuitable (e.g. polluted) people to keep away, but here the conventional phrase underlines with grim irony the abnormality (and pollution) of the 'sacrifice' itself (the kind of act from which all would wish to keep their distance).[16] The comparison of infanticide to sacrificial killing represents a shocking perversion of ritual norms, yet it conveys Medea's consciously self-destructive stance. Thus when she declares, 'My hand will not weaken' (1055), the audience know that if Medea should kill her own children, it will be a deliberate and violent negation of her innermost self and affections. One side of her moral sense, her sensitivity to dishonour, will have obliterated another, her duty (and love) as a parent.

However, as she renews her determination for the deed, Medea is overcome once again by doubts. Addressing her own heart (*thumos*), she urges it to spare the children, and even imagines taking them with her to Athens to gladden her life there (1056-8; cf. 1045). Yet this idea is immediately and powerfully overturned, creating the most forceful disjunction in the entire speech, as Medea suddenly moves from imagining the children alive in Athens to picturing their humiliation by her enemies in Corinth (1059-61).[17] Unable to bear the thought of her enemies taking revenge, Medea finally convinces herself that the death of her children is 'necessary' (1060).[18] Rather than being a calculated rationalisation of her act,[19] Medea's feeling of necessity is both agonising and psychologically compelling: Creon's daughter has received the poison and there is no going back.[20] Before the children go into the house for the last time, Medea embraces them, and her sensual pleasure in their bodies ('O sweet embrace, O soft skin and sweet breath of my children!', 1074-5) enhances the agony of her decision. Finally, as she orders the children inside, Medea acknowledges the consciously self-destructive nature of her actions (1078-80):

> I know what evil deeds I am about to do,
> but my anger is in charge of my plans,
> anger which causes the greatest evils for mortals.

These lines have been the subject of intense debate, particularly 1079, which has often been translated 'but my anger is stronger than my [rational] plans'. On this traditional view, Medea is taken to be stating the familiar (Platonic) opposition of reason versus passion.[21] In other words, Medea knows what it is right to do (i.e. not kill her children), but her *thumos* (anger / desire for revenge) overwhelms her reason (or 'plans', *bouleumata*).[22] However, many scholars have recently queried the traditional model of (moral) reason versus (non-moral) passion, with passion proving triumphant.[23] As one critic observes, 'ethical reasons, as well as feelings, underlie each of the positions that make up Medea's dilemma, including the position identified with *thumos*'.[24] On this view, Medea's *bouleumata* are her 'revenge plans', not her reasoning powers,[25] and *kreissôn* has the sense 'is in charge of / is master of' instead of 'is stronger than'. Moreover, Medea's *thumos* is rightly seen to refer to something wider than (non-moral) 'passion', for the word *thumos* (whose semantic range includes 'heart', 'anger', 'pride', and 'self-esteem') here expresses Medea's heroic pride and its accompanying ethic of revenge.[26] And it is Medea's own awareness of the cost of her *thumos* to herself (in killing her children she destroys what she holds dearest) which makes her revenge particularly stirring and tragic.

The Chorus grasp Medea's intentions and react in chanted anapaests, declaring that people who have no children are more fortunate than those who do (1090ff.). The Chorus' troubled response focuses our attention on the impending infanticide, but Euripides prolongs the suspense by having the first part of Medea's revenge, the deaths of Creon and his daughter, reported to her in a lengthy messenger speech. Whereas Medea had ended her great speech in a mood of sorrow for her children, her tone now changes to *Schadenfreude* as she relishes the news of her enemies' destruction (cf. 1134-5, 'You will give me twice as much pleasure if they died most horribly').[27] The Messenger's account is indeed horrific as first Jason's new bride and then her father are killed by the flesh-eating robe and crown. Medea had lamented the lost marriage rituals of her sons and their absence from her funeral (cf. 1022-6, 1032-5), but here she combines both events (marriage and death) and fashions a fatal wedding for Creon's daughter. The grisly details of the girl's death evoke sympathy, complicating further the audience's response to Medea's revenge, a process begun by the declaration of infanticide (792-3) and intensified in the final scene. When the Messenger has finished his description of the deaths, he turns to Medea's fate, and his words ('You will soon know yourself the punishment to come', 1223) have an added meaning for the audience, since they know that Medea's 'punishment' will be both consciously chosen and self-inflicted, and that it will also be the final stage of her revenge.

The Chorus react to the death of Jason's new relatives in terms that are extremely significant for our response to the rest of the play: 'It seems that some god has justly fastened many disasters upon Jason this day' (1231-2; cf. 1208). For they regard Jason's suffering as not only *justified* but also as an instance of *divine punishment*. And it is precisely these two features, the justice of Medea's revenge and its relation to the gods, which will be the focus of interest in the final scene. Just before Medea enters the house, she restates her decision to kill the children within. The core arguments of her great monologue are repeated in quick succession (1236-41), creating an atmosphere of urgency as the climax of the play approaches. Medea describes the infanticide itself as a 'terrible and necessary evil' (1243), and her form of self-address ('But come, my heart, put on your armour!', 1242) illustrates the heroic ethos that makes even such a heart-rending revenge 'necessary'. Medea's last words before the murder are especially poignant: she urges herself to forget for one day how much she loves her children, and foresees her future life as one of permanent grief and pain (1245-50). The personal cost of her revenge could not be expressed more forcefully or pitifully.

As Medea enters the house, the Chorus sing their final stasimon, a frantic appeal to the gods to prevent the murder of the children. Invoking Helios, Medea's grandfather, the Chorus beg him to save his great-grandchildren (1255-7), but their appeal goes unanswered. Still more disturbingly, when Helios does intervene, it is to give Medea the divine chariot with which she escapes after the murders (1321-2). In this way the Chorus' invocation introduces an idea which will dominate the final scene: the distance between human and divine approaches to justice. From the Chorus' mortal perspective, the problem with Medea's revenge is not the target (the guilty Jason) but the means (the innocent children). However, as Medea's god-like actions show, divine vengeance may involve destroying the innocent as well as the guilty. While the death of Creon and his daughter was narrated in a messenger speech, we actually hear the screams of the children from inside the house (1271-2, 1277-8), and their death cries create one of the most visceral and shocking moments in Greek tragedy. The Chorus' response underlines the unique horror of Medea's act, as they claim to have heard of only one parallel to her crime, the child-killer Ino.[28] However, unlike Ino, whom the Chorus describe as 'driven mad by the gods' (1284), Medea intentionally murders her children, and her sane calculation makes her act far more disturbing.[29] Moreover, whereas Ino's infanticide involved her own death (1286-9), Medea appears god-like and triumphant and escapes alive to Athens.

The final scene confronts Jason with the consequences of his treachery and explores the gap between divine and human standards of justice. When Jason arrives from the palace, he looks forward to Medea's punishment by the royal family, but is more concerned that its vengeance may fall upon his sons (1296-305). Both predictions prove false: Medea has already used the children as instruments of her own revenge, while her appearance in the Chariot of the Sun enables her to escape the retribution of the Corinthians.[30] In the eyes of the Chorus Jason's ignorance is pitiful: 'Poor man, you do not know, Jason, how far into evils you have come. For otherwise you would not have said these words' (1306-7). When the Chorus tell him of the infanticide, Jason is 'destroyed' by their words (1310; cf. 1326), and we see him in the sympathetic role of the grieving parent, but one who, unlike Medea, refuses to accept his share of responsibility for the children's death.[31] As Jason orders the doors to be opened, Medea's theatrically stunning appearance above the house in the Chariot of the Sun powerfully expresses her new status as a quasi-divine avenger.[32] Both her location and her language ('Cease from this labour of yours! [i.e. to unbar the doors]', 1319) emphasise the transcendence of divine power.[33]

Jason is unwilling to recognise the gods' complicity in Medea's revenge and reviles her as 'most hateful to the gods' (1323-4). He is also unable to accept that he is being punished for *his* betrayal, and, alluding to Medea's murder of her brother Apsyrtus, he claims that he is suffering for *her* crime ('the gods have sent your spirit of vengeance against me', 1333). As Jason confronts his ruined life, he blames Medea's excessive anger 'for the sake of a bed and marriage' (1338; cf. 1366, Chapter 2), but the audience understand the importance of his broken pledge. Nevertheless, Jason is right to pinpoint the self-destructiveness of Medea's conduct, and their angry dialogue forcefully expresses the dilemma of her 'heroic' revenge (1360-2):

> *Medea*: I have stung your heart, just as I had to do.
> *Jason*: But you too suffer and share in these evils.
> *Medea*: You are right, but the grief is worthwhile if you cannot laugh at me.

Viewed from Jason's perspective, Medea's act seems evil and irrational, but its psychological and moral impact upon the audience are crucially altered (and complicated) by her emergence as a god-like avenger. Significantly, Medea responds to Jason's accusations of impiety and pollution by implying that Zeus, king of the gods, approves of her revenge: 'I would have made a long speech in reply to these words of yours, if father Zeus did not know how you were treated by me and what you did in return' (1351-3). Moreover, as Jason and Medea exchange reproaches (1363ff.), they continue to dispute the attitude of the gods to the infanticide (1372-3): when Medea claims, 'The gods know who began the torment', Jason retorts, 'Yes, they know indeed your abominable spirit.'

Nevertheless, the issue of divine support is prevented from becoming a mere stalemate argument between an alienated couple. For Medea herself escapes like a goddess, while her last major speech has the characteristics of a concluding *deus ex machina* pronouncement:[34] she institutes a new festival and cult to atone for her children's murder (1381-3) and prophesies the ignominious death of Jason himself (1386-8).[35] The aetiology and function of the children's cult are particularly interesting.

4. Medea's Revenge

Medea's children were indeed honoured with a festival at the shrine of Hera Akraia in the fifth century BC, but it was regarded as a ritual of atonement instituted by the Corinthians.[36] Moreover, its function was almost certainly to make amends for the murder of the children by the Corinthians themselves.[37] The function of the historical ritual was thus crucially different from that established by Medea – and naturally so, if Euripides invented the children's deliberate murder by their own mother. In other words, we see Euripides retaining a basic feature of the historical cult (its expiatory purpose), but inventing a new aetiology to fit his version of the myth.[38] Medea recognises the guilt of her 'unholy murder' (1383) and alleviates the stain of pollution by establishing compensatory rites in the children's honour.[39] Finally, and no less importantly, Medea's institution of such a cult confirms not only her god-like power but also her continuing love for her children.

Medea's revenge and escape are especially disturbing because they seem to imply divine complicity with child-murder. Though the gods do not explicitly motivate Medea's revenge, neither do they intervene or subsequently punish her, and the audience is left to assume that they endorse (or are indifferent to) her actions. Given Medea's numerous invocations of Zeus, Themis, and Dike (Justice), and the repeated emphasis on divine oaths (cf. 1391-2), the audience are encouraged to see Jason's punishment as a religious duty.[40] Yet while Medea punishes Jason's impiety with genuinely divine harshness, there is (as often in Euripides) a focus on the problematic aspects of such divine severity.[41] Moreover, the conflict between human and divine approaches to justice has here a particularly shocking impact, since Medea's god-like revenge is simultaneously a violation of the most fundamental human ties, the relationship between parent and child.[42]

The murder of her children, combined with her seemingly triumphant escape, has led many critics to view Medea as ultimately 'dehumanised' or 'demonised' by her actions.[43] Jason condemns her as a 'lioness, not a woman, with a nature more savage than the Tyrrhenian monster Scylla!' (1342-3; cf. 1407), but his images of wildness and monstrosity are belied by Medea's authentic human grief. Similarly, although the Chorus present Medea as an Erinys (or Fury, 1259-60), and Medea herself swears by 'Hades' underworld avengers' (1059), we should not forget that the Greeks viewed the Furies as agents of divine justice, and it would therefore be unwise to consider Medea's revenge 'demonic' in a purely negative sense. It is also significant that Medea's transformation is *not* an apotheosis which brings freedom from mortal cares, for although she will escape to Athens, she cannot escape a life of human mourning. While Medea's god-like perspective in the final scene alters the impact of her revenge, it is her mortal viewpoint which has dominated most of the action, and we do not simply forget that she has suffered as a mortal woman and mother, and will continue to do so, despite her superhuman escape.[44]

The tragedy of Medea's revenge is that in punishing her enemy she destroys those who are dearest to her. But although the infanticide is a shocking perversion of the moral code of 'helping friends and harming enemies' (voiced by Medea herself: 809-10), the audience cannot dismiss her act as merely 'inhuman' or 'demonic'. Furthermore, as we saw in Chapter 2, the (largely male) Athenian audience is brought to realise not only Jason's share of responsibility for the deaths, but also how Medea's status as a woman forces her to exact retribution within her own *oikos*.[45] No ordinary Athenian woman could so punish her husband and escape, and there is thus a critical point to Medea's god-like authority in the final scene, for her power as the granddaughter of Helios underlines her powerlessness as a woman.[46]

It is no small part of the play's ongoing fascination that it makes us comprehend how a loving mother could commit such an appalling crime. In addition, our understanding of the ethical principles underpinning Medea's revenge means that we do not lose sympathy with her entirely, even when she kills her children.[47] Thus perhaps the greatest challenge to our preconceptions is that we are brought to see a child-killer as 'a human being, not a monster'.[48] Finally, though Medea's vengeance is shocking, it is also an expression of divine justice (compare the matricide in *Electra*), and the audience is forced to confront (and make sense of) such an ethical universe.[49] As a result the closing scene is both powerfully moving and disturbing, for it combines Medea's god-like impunity with her continuing human pain, and her ruthless punishment of her enemy with her self-destructive, and deeply tragic, revenge.

5

Multi-Medea

Despite winning only the third prize at the City Dionysia of 431 BC, *Medea* has proved to be one of the most popular and influential of all Greek tragedies.[1] A comprehensive history of the play's reception in literature, music, and art is far beyond the scope of this book,[2] and this chapter will consider only some of the most notable examples, concentrating on literature of the classical period.

The earliest literary reference to *Medea* comes in Aristophanes' *Women at the Thesmophoria*, which was performed at the City Dionysia in 411 BC. In a parody of previous Euripidean plots (especially *Helen* and *Andromeda*) the Aristophanic 'Euripides' is forced to undertake a daring rescue mission; when he is confronted by a dim barbarian archer, Euripides adapts a line from his earlier play, 'For if you offer clever new ideas to the stupid, you'll be wasting your efforts' (*Thesmophoriazusae* 1130-1; *Medea* 298-9). Leaving aside the question of *Medea*'s influence on Neophron's play of the same name (probably dated to the fourth century BC: see Chapter 1), we learn from Aristotle (*Rhetoric* 1400b) that the tragic poet Carcinus, who was working in Athens from the 370s onwards, wrote a *Medea* 'in which Medea was *falsely accused* of killing her children'.[3] Unfortunately, we do not know how Carcinus presented the children's death (he may have used the older story in which the children die accidentally while being made immortal), but it is clear in any case that he aimed to handle the myth very differently from Euripides.

Turning for a moment from literature to art, the choice of scenes on western Greek vase-painting from the late fifth century BC onwards illustrates not only the popularity of tragedy, especially Euripidean tragedy, well beyond Athens, but also the particular impact of *Medea* itself.[4] It is striking that the two episodes which seem to have appealed most to the vase-painters' imagination are also the theatrical highpoints of the play: the murder of the children (not seen on stage in Euripides' version, but heard to such great effect that the audience can visualise the killing inside the house) and Medea's escape on the Chariot of the Sun. The earliest of these south Italian vases (*c*. 400 BC) both depict Medea's supernatural departure upon the snake-drawn chariot.[5] Significantly, however, the vase-painters have in each case diverged from Euripides' play to suit their own artistic ends, and show Medea leaving her children's bodies behind for Jason to bury, making her superhuman status even more emphatic. Similarly, on the three south Italian vases from later in the fourth century which show the infanticide (nos. 29-31, *c*. 330 BC), the artists have elaborated on the basic scene (one includes, for example, the death of Creon's daughter in the upper part of the painting), but their debt to Euripides' version of the myth is clear.

As we saw in Chapter 1, Medea's relationship with Jason is part of the larger myth of the Argonauts' quest for the Golden Fleece, and while some early poets focused on Jason and Medea's first meeting in Colchis (cf. Hesiod, *Theogony* 992-1002, Pindar *Pythian* 4.213-23), Euripides chose to portray the tragic consequences of their broken marriage back in Greece. With Apollonius' epic *Argonautica*, written around the middle of the third century BC, we return to the earlier stages of the myth, yet his poem shows a constant awareness of Euripides' development of the story.[6] Although the great popularity of *Medea* made it an influential model for all subsequent treatments, the tendency to intertextual engagement with earlier literature was

particularly strong in the case of Alexandrian poetry.[7] Throughout his work Apollonius skilfully exploits his audience's
familiarity with Euripides' play, showing 'how the origins of the
tragedy lay far back, [while] the tragedy lends deep resonance
and "tragic" irony to the events of the epic'.[8]

Apollonius' poem, composed in four books, begins with Pelias'
initial challenge to Jason (1.1-22) and ends with the Argonauts'
successful return to Greece (4.1773-81). But insofar as the epic
supplies the 'back-story', as it were, to Euripides' play, it is
Books 3 and 4 which are particularly significant, since they
present Medea falling in love with Jason, betraying her father
and brother to help him, and finally abandoning her homeland
for Greece. Medea, the priestess of Hecate in Colchis (3.252; cf.
Medea 395-8), is described by Hera as 'full of cunning' (3.89,
Medea 401-2). When Eros makes her fall passionately in love
with Jason, Medea is torn between ignoring Jason's plight and
so seeing him die, or helping him and thereby disgracing herself
among the Colchians (3.771-801), and her monologue recalls the
Euripidean Medea's anguished speech before her final determination upon infanticide (*Medea* 1040-80). Jason's dependence
on Medea is repeatedly emphasised (cf. *Medea* 476-87), as is
both his debt to her as a suppliant (3.985-9, *Medea* 496-8) and
his solemn oath to respect her as his lawful wife (4.92-8, *Medea*
160-3). Thus, by using his audience's knowledge of the later
history of Jason and Medea's relationship, Apollonius creates
an atmosphere of ominous and tragic foreboding: Medea's accusations of ingratitude, in the belief that Jason is about to
abandon her, prefigure her real betrayal in Corinth (4.355-90,
Medea 499-510).[9] Most strikingly, when Medea's brother, Apsyrtus, is lured by her to his death, he is compared to a child (4.460),
and his killing foreshadows the murder of Medea's own children
(cf. 4.1108-9).

As the Romans appropriated Greek culture for their own
ends, the impact of Euripides' *Medea* was felt in various genres

of Latin literature. Not surprisingly, however, the play's influence was most conspicuous in the field of Latin tragedy. Adaptations of Greek tragedies (especially the works of Euripides) were being performed at Roman public festivals from 240 BC onwards, and each of the major early Latin tragedians (Ennius, Pacuvius, and Accius) adapted the Medea myth for the Roman stage.[10] While Pacuvius' *Medus*[11] and Accius' *Medea* (or *Argonauts*)[12] dealt with events beyond Corinth, Ennius' *Medea* is a close adaptation of Euripides' play.[13] The first nine lines of Ennius' tragedy (fr. CIII Jocelyn) allow us to see him adapting the first eight lines of Euripides in a free manner, reversing the *hysteron proteron* in the original Greek,[14] and giving a novel etymology of the name *Argo* (so called because the *Argives* sailed in it). The surviving fragments of *Medea* (like those of his *Hecuba* and *Iphigenia in Aulis*) show Ennius transforming the Greek original to suit the language and customs of his Roman audience: Medea addresses the female Corinthian Chorus as *matronae opulentae optumates* ('wealthy noble matrons', fr. CV(a)) and invokes Jupiter instead of Earth (fr. CX; *Medea* 1251ff.).

Latin authors continued to write tragedies based on Greek myths throughout the Republican period and well into the first century AD. In 29 BC Varius Rufus' *Thyestes* was performed at the Roman games celebrating the battle of Actium, and Augustus' reign also saw the production of Ovid's *Medea*,[15] which Tacitus (*Dialogus* 12) and Quintilian (*Institutio oratoria* 10.1.98) describe as being both popular and a work of genius.[16] Unfortunately, only two verses from Ovid's tragedy survive.[17] However, Ovid portrays Medea at length elsewhere (principally in *Heroides* 12 and *Metamorphoses* 7.1-424),[18] and it is tempting to see in these treatments, with their emphasis on Medea's passionate love turned to anger (*Heroides* 12.135-58, 207-12) and their foregrounding of Medea's magical powers (*Metamorphoses* 7.179-293), some of the main themes of his *Medea*. After his banishment by Augustus in AD 8 to Tomis on the Black Sea, Ovid continued to write poetry, but his focus on Medea shifts to her experience as an exile. In *Tristia* ('Sorrows') 3.8.3-4, for example, the exiled poet wishes for the dragon-drawn chariot with which Medea had once escaped from Corinth.[19]

Though Ovid's tragedy is lost, the *Medea* of Seneca has survived complete.[20] Seneca's drama, dated to around the middle of the first century AD, resembles Euripides' play in both situation and plot: the setting is Corinth and Medea is shown forming and subsequently enacting her horrific revenge. Nevertheless, Seneca's handling of the story diverges from Euripides' *Medea* in several important respects, giving his tragedy a unique atmosphere and impact. When the play begins, for example, Jason's wedding to Creon's daughter is still taking place (37-9, 299-300; contrast *Medea* 18-19), yet Medea is already plotting death for Creon and his daughter and 'something worse [than death]' for Jason himself (17-20). While Medea blames Creon more than Jason for her abandonment and divorce (137-8), she argues that Jason is equally guilty of Pelias' death (275-80).[21] When her arguments fail, Medea supplicates Creon (282ff.), as in Euripides' play (324ff.), and gains an extra day with her children.[22] Significantly, Jason's love for the children is more prominent in Seneca, motivating Medea's choice of punishment more directly (544-50), while altering the balance of sympathy between the parents. Moreover, in contrast to Euripides' Corinthian women, Seneca's Chorus remain hostile to Medea throughout (cf. 361-3, 870-3).

It is in the final scene (879-1027), however, that the individuality of Seneca's version is most marked. For although Seneca's protagonist, like Euripides', delivers a lengthy monologue in which she is torn between the contradictory impulses of vengeance and love for her children, whom she embraces (893-947, *Medea* 1021ff.), the act of killing is presented in a wholly original manner. As Medea seeks to strengthen her determination for the deed, the Furies suddenly appear together with the ghost of her brother Apsyrtus, whose murder by Medea they seek to avenge (957-66, cf. *Medea* 1333-5). Medea thus kills the first of her sons to appease her brother's Furies, offering the child as a sacrificial victim (967-71) and murdering him on stage (contrast *Medea* 1271ff., where the children's screams are heard from inside the house).[23] Carrying the child's corpse, Medea leads her remaining son up on to the roof of the house and kills him there, rejecting Jason's offer to die in his place (1004-19). Finally, as Medea escapes on the snake-drawn chariot, she leaves the children's bodies behind for Jason to bury (1024, contrast her careful institution of cult in *Medea* 1378-83).[24] As a result of these differences Seneca's Medea seems a less recognisably human and sympathetic figure than her Euripidean counterpart,[25] but it would be unfair to call Seneca's treatment of the myth 'melodramatic' rather than 'tragic',[26] since his Medea is still aware of the self-destructive nature of her vengeful anger (926-32), even if such knowledge is finally overshadowed by her delight at Jason's ruin and her pride in her own malevolence (986-94).[27]

Ever since the Renaissance, when the texts of the surviving Greek tragedies re-emerged from obscurity, Euripides' *Medea* has played a central role in the rebirth of Greek tragedy as a performance genre. The huge number and variety of modern productions and adaptations of *Medea* testify to its enduring dramatic power and relevance.[28] Moreover, it has not only been dramatists such as Pierre Corneille in 1630s France[29] or Heiner Müller in 1980s Germany[30] who have felt the pull of the myth, for Medea has also appeared throughout the centuries in numerous operas, ballets, paintings, novels, and films. Since the history of the myth's reception has attracted a great deal of attention in recent years (see n. 2), I shall briefly mention only two examples from the fields of cinema and the novel.

Pier Paolo Pasolini's film *Medea* (1970) constructs a clear division between the 'primitive', 'natural' world of Colchis, where humans are sacrificed and their blood sprinkled upon the earth to increase its fertility, and the 'ordered', 'civilised' city of Corinth, where Medea is shunned as a dangerous foreign witch.[31] Shaping the myth in these terms, Pasolini exploits the polarity in a way that is critical of modern (rationalistic and bourgeois) society: 'The antique ... world of Colchis represents an ideal of harmony, where everything is sacred, because the category of the "desecrated" has not been introduced by repression and alienation. For Pasolini's Medea, "nothing more" is possible in the contaminated, repressed modern world for which Jason and Corinth stand.'[32] Pasolini's film follows the Euripidean story-pattern quite closely, especially at its climax: Medea kills her sons to punish Jason. By contrast, Christa Wolf's novel *Medea* (1996)[33] presents a different (and possibly pre-Euripidean: cf. Chapter 1) version of the infanticide, for here the Corinthians kill the children and then spread a rumour that Medea murdered them herself.[34] Indeed, Medea is equally innocent of the deaths of Apsyrtus and Glauce (Creon's daughter): Apsyrtus is murdered by the Colchians in a ritual of human sacrifice, while Glauce kills herself by jumping into a well. Moreover, the so-called 'civilised' city of Corinth contains a dark secret, for Creon has sacrificed his eldest daughter (Iphinoe) to preserve his power and keeps her skeleton in a chamber beneath the palace. Yet despite these differences, Wolf explores a number of issues which are fundamental to Euripides' play: the corrupting effects of political power and ambition (both Aeëtes and Creon sacrifice their own children to secure their thrones, while Jason acquiesces in the scapegoating of his former wife), the unfair treatment of women (Jason is puzzled by the respect given to women in Colchis), and the ease with which outsiders become a target for revenge (Medea is joined in Corinth by a group of Colchian refugees, who are also attacked by the Corinthian mob).

As was noted above, Greek tragedy has become, in the last thirty years especially, a truly international art-form, with performances of *Medea* taking place throughout the world. Moreover, there is no such thing as a definitive production, and while this book has sought primarily to discuss the *Medea* in its original socio-cultural and poetic context, each society and age will approach the play with a specific set of values and concerns, and so perform it in a unique (and uniquely revealing) manner. As one scholar has observed, while comparing Euripides' dramatic art to Shakespeare's, both poets concentrate on 'putting a part of life in its entire complexity, richness, and depth on the stage'.[35] And with *Medea*, which combines moral complexity with an overwhelming emotional impact, Euripides has succeeded in creating not only one of the most powerful figures in all of Greek literature but also one of its greatest tragic dramas.

Notes

1. Festival, Myth, and Play

1. For an excellent introduction to the Athenian Dionysia and a translation of the ancient evidence, see Csapo and Slater, *The Context of Ancient Drama*, 103-21. (For books and articles referred to by short titles, see the Guide to Further Reading.)

2. See A.W. Pickard-Cambridge, *Dramatic Festivals*, 58-9.

3. Pickard-Cambridge, *Dramatic Festivals*, 263-5.

4. Csapo and Slater, *The Context of Ancient Drama*, 286-93.

5. E. Hall, 'The Sociology of Athenian Tragedy', in P.E. Easterling (ed.), *The Cambridge Companion to Greek Tragedy*, 93-126, p. 95.

6. For a recent defence of a circular Athenian *orchêstra* in the fifth century, see D. Wiles, *Tragedy in Athens: Performance Space and Theatrical Meaning* (Cambridge: Cambridge University Press, 1997), 44-52.

7. J.-C. Moretti, 'The Theater of the Sanctuary of Dionysus Eleuthereus in Late Fifth-Century Athens', *Illinois Classical Studies* 24-5 (1999-2000), 377-98, p. 392.

8. Cf. e.g. Csapo and Slater, *The Context of Ancient Drama*, 80 (pro-stage, at least from the 420s onwards); anti-stage: Wiles (n. 6), 63-5.

9. For the development of this 'liturgy' (or 'public work'), see P.J. Wilson, *The Athenian Institution of the Khoregia* (Cambridge: Cambridge University Press, 2000).

10. Page, *Medea*, xxxi claims that *Medea* was performed with only two actors. However, such a division would seem to overburden the performers and is found in no other surviving Euripidean tragedy. Moreover, the opening scene actually demands three speaking actors (the Nurse and Paidagogos on stage, Medea inside the house): cf. 89-105.

11. Contrast the vocal on-stage children of *Alcestis* 393-415, *Andromache* 504-36, and *Suppliant Women* 1123-61.

12. For discussion of the fragments and a conjectural reconstruction of the plays, see T.B.L. Webster, *The Tragedies of Euripides* (London: Methuen, 1967), 57-64.

13. According to a scholion (a critical note in our manuscripts often derived from ancient commentaries) on *Medea* 9, the tale was recorded by the Hellenistic grammarian Parmeniscus.

14. The Iolcus cycle is one of four separate mythical narratives that make up the subject matter of most early Greek heroic poetry, the others being the Aetolian-Elean-Pylian cycle, the Theban cycle, and the (to us most familiar, because described by Homer) Trojan cycle: see M.L. West, *The Hesiodic Catalogue of Women* (Oxford: Oxford University Press, 1985), 137-8.

15. The earliest surviving depiction of Medea (*c.* 630 BC) shows just such a rejuvenation scene. It also comes from an Etruscan vase, showing the widespread diffusion of the myth even by this time: cf. C.J. Smith, 'Barter and Exchange in the Archaic Mediterranean', in G.R. Tsetskhladze (ed.), *Ancient Greeks West and East* (Leiden: Brill, 1999), 179-206, pp. 197-202.

16. Cf. e.g. *LIMC*, 'Pelias', nos. 10-11. (For abbreviations, see the Guide to Further Reading.) The Pelias episode is the most popular scene on vases dealing with the Medea myth before 431 BC: cf. V. Zinserling-Paul, 'Zum Bild der Medea in der antiken Kunst', *Klio* 61 (1979), 407-36, pp. 411-23, C. Sourvinou-Inwood, 'Medea at a Shifting Distance', in Clauss and Johnston (eds), *Medea*, 253-96, pp. 262-6. The sixth-century BC lyric poet Stesichorus wrote a work called *The Funeral Games of Pelias* (frs 178-80 *PMG*).

17. Jason's name means 'healer'. C.J. Mackie, 'The Earliest Jason: What's in a Name?', *Greece and Rome* 48 (2001), 1-17, p. 2 argues persuasively 'that it is Jason who may have possessed powers of healing and skills in mixing drugs in the very earliest narratives', and that these skills were subsequently transferred to the barbarian Medea: cf. Chapter 3.

18. As D.L. Cairns (ed.), *Oxford Readings in Homer's Iliad* (Oxford: Oxford University Press, 2001), 17 points out in an illuminating discussion of divine intervention in epic, the situation is actually more complex than this approach might suggest since 'ascriptions of responsibility to gods or humans are at the mercy of the speaker's intention in context'. So here the rhetorical intention of the speaker (Jason) is foiled by the audience's knowledge of Medea's crucial and deliberate decision to help Jason.

19. Since Aeschylus died in 456, his *Argo* predated *Peliades*, but we know very little about the play. A.H. Sommerstein, *Aeschylean Tragedy* (Bari: Levante, 1993), 60-1 suggests that it may have been the satyr-play of Aeschylus' Argonautic trilogy *The Lemnian Women, Cabeiroi, Hypsipyle*. In this case the focus is more likely to have been on the

Argonauts' visit to Lemnos than on Jason's return to Iolcus with Medea.

20. For a reconstruction of the plot, see Webster (n. 12), 32-6.

21. Cf. A.C. Pearson, *The Fragments of Sophocles* (Cambridge: Cambridge University Press, 1917), vol. 2, 172-7.

22. Cf. fr. 343 R, Pearson (n. 21) vol. 2, 15-23.

23. See Webster (n. 12), 77-80.

24. Similarly, with regard to Sophocles' *Aegeus*, Pearson (n. 21) vol. 1, 15 thought it 'probable that the *anagnôrisis* ["recognition"] of Theseus formed the climax of the action'.

25. Webster (n. 12), 52-3.

26. For the following, cf. frs 2-3 *EGF*, scholion to Pindar, *Olympian* 13.74, Pausanias 2.3.11.

27. Scholars dispute whether the Creophylus concerned is the seventh-century BC epic poet from Samos or the fourth-century BC historian from Ephesus; cf. M. Davies, 'Deianeira and Medea: A Footnote to the Pre-History of Two Myths', *Mnemosyne* 42 (1989), 469-72, pp. 470-1.

28. S.I. Johnston, 'Corinthian Medea and the Cult of Hera Akraia', in Clauss and Johnston (eds), *Medea*, 44-70, p. 45, for example, argues that 'fifth-century authors inherited an infanticidal Medea from myth'. However, J. March, *Classical Review* 49 (1999), 362 criticises Johnston's theory that Medea was already established as an infanticidal demon in early Greek thought: 'This simply does not work. Medea never kills other women's children, and even when she murders her own in Euripides, she is an all-too-human mother who grieves even as she kills them.' It may be significant that no surviving vase predating Euripides' play shows Medea killing her children, whereas after 431 BC this becomes the scene most often depicted.

29. Page, *Medea*, xxx-xxxvi. Less patiently, U. von Wilamowitz-Moellendorff, 'Exkurse zu Euripides Medeia', *Hermes* 15 (1880), 481-523, p. 487 claimed that the whole Neophron story was merely a 'malicious, tendentious, Peloponnesian forgery'. (Neophron came from Sicyon, near Corinth, which also claimed to have invented tragedy.)

30. Cf. E.A. Thompson, 'Neophron and Euripides' *Medea*', *Classical Quarterly* 38 (1944), 10-14, B. Manuwald, 'Der Mord an den Kindern', *Wiener Studien* 17 (1983), 27-61, A.N. Michelini, 'Neophron and Euripides' *Medea* 1056-80', *Transactions of the American Philological Association* 119 (1989), 115-35.

31. Thompson (n. 30), 14 thinks it 'unlikely' that a later Neophron would have dared to handle such a well known myth, but there is much evidence of dramatists returning again and again to popular story-patterns (cf. e.g. Aeschylus, *Choephori*, Sophocles, *Electra*, Euripides, *Electra*). Michelini (n. 30), 127 claims 'it is evident that Euripides' [speech, i.e. 1042-80] adapted the switch in voices from Neophron'. But it could just as well have been the other way round.

32. Besides the stylistic arguments made by Page (n. 29), one notes the many similarities between the monologues of the two Medeas, where each heroine addresses both her own heart and her children. The dramatic brilliance of the soliloquy in Euripides' version suggests that Neophron is drawing on an already famous scene. In addition, Neophron's Medea seems to rehearse the major themes of Euripides' play (e.g. 'friend' versus 'enemy', Medea's wilfulness) rather too mechanically.

33. That is, the significance of Medea's actions is scarcely exhausted by the question of their invention.

34. In the *Poetics* Aristotle says that the dramatist should *visualise* his material as much as possible while writing his plays (1455a22-6). Similarly, when reading the text, we should always try to picture the events on stage, bearing in mind that the texts we read are first and foremost scripts for *performance*.

35. I use the Oxford Classical Text, edited by J. Diggle (Oxford University Press, 1984). My main disagreement concerns the deletion of a large part of Medea's monologue (1056-80); see Chapter 4.

36. Euripides' plays generally begin with an introductory speech of this kind, sometimes delivered by a god (*Alcestis, Hippolytus, Trojan Women, Ion, Bacchae*); the two exceptions are thought by many to be non-Euripidean: *Rhesus* and the (first) prologue-scene of *Iphigenia in Aulis* (1-48).

37. In Aristophanes' *Frogs* (948-52) Euripides boasts that he gave a voice to slaves in the name of democracy.

38. Cf. B. Gredley, 'The Place and Time of Victory: Euripides' *Medea*', *Bulletin of the Institute of Classical Studies* 34 (1987), 27-39, p. 28: 'Medea's cries are themselves unusual, since utterances from "within" normally enact a violent climax of action; here they accurately prefigure the murder of the children (1270ff.).'

39. The use of the same metre suggests the strong emotional attachment between Medea and the Nurse.

40. Apart from the central double-door of the *skênê*, actors and chorus could also enter and exit along the two side-entrances (*eisodoi*) at either side of the performance area. The directions represented by these entrance ramps differ from play to play, but once identified by the action they remain the same throughout. Here one leads to Corinth and the royal palace, while the other (used only by Aegeus) represents the country roads to and from Corinth.

41. C. W. Willink, 'Euripides' *Medea* 1-45, 371-85', *Classical Quarterly* 38 (1988), 313-23, p. 323.

42. G.M.A. Grube, *The Drama of Euripides* (London: Methuen, 1941), 151.

43. Gredley (n. 38), 27.

44. Creon himself admits that he is making a mistake (350-1), a surprising remark which arouses curiosity about the consequences of his error.

45. Such songs are called *stasima* (or 'songs in position') because they were delivered after the chorus had entered the *orchêstra*.

46. The first four stasima of *Medea* share a similar metrical form (strophe and antistrophe in dactylo-epitrites, followed by a second strophic pair in aeolo-choriambics): cf. A.M. Dale, *The Lyric Metres of Greek Drama* (Cambridge: Cambridge University Press, 1968²), 180. Strikingly, however, the pattern breaks down in the fifth stasimon as the infanticide draws near (see on 1251-92 below).

47. This fundamental revision of women's reputation is marked by other startling reversals in the fabric of the world: 'The streams of holy rivers flow uphill; everything, even justice, is overturned' (410-11).

48. A type of rhetorical set-piece found in most Euripidean trage-dies; see M. Lloyd, *The Agon in Euripides* (Oxford: Oxford University Press, 1992), 1-18.

49. For similarly overt rhetorical markers, cf. *Hippolytus* 991-3, *Hecuba* 1195-6, *Electra* 1060, *Heracles* 174-6, *Trojan Women* 916-17.

50. Lloyd (n. 48), 43, who also notes that Jason's rhetorical skill 'is not balanced by any appropriate emotional response or moral judge-ment, and his speech seems correspondingly shallow'.

51. For the metrical scheme, see Dale (n. 46), 185, 192.

52. Cf. P. Sfyroeras, 'The Ironies of Salvation: The Aegeus Scene in Euripides' *Medea*', *Classical Journal* 90 (1994), 125-42, pp. 125-6 for a sample of such criticisms.

53. Easterling, 'Infanticide', 184.

54. D. Kovacs, 'Zeus in Euripides' *Medea*', *American Journal of Philology* 114 (1993), 45-70, p. 58 discusses the scene on another level as a 'coincidence brought about by the gods', an instance of divine *tychê* ('fortune', 'chance') intended to punish Jason.

55. As the audience are aware, Aegeus will go on to father the Athenian hero Theseus in Troezen. Medea does not disclose the oracle's not-so-cryptic meaning (do not have sex before reaching Athens) as this would be hard to reconcile with the traditional myth of Theseus' birth. Perhaps Euripides invented the oracle here precisely to under-line the pain of childlessness? In any case, given the nature of the oracle's reply (679-81), there are some who find the scene comic and Aegeus ridiculous. Though this seems to exaggerate the scene's comic element, a wry smile at Aegeus' puzzlement does seem likely. (Perhaps there is even a secondary level of humour in the oracle's 'wineskin', since Pittheus, king of Troezen, is said to have got Aegeus drunk before having him sleep with his daughter Aethra.) Nevertheless, such humour as there is has a serious purpose, for it throws into relief the genuine misery of Aegeus' lack of offspring.

56. It is significant for an Athenian audience's response that one of their mythical kings express such a clear judgement.

57. It is often alleged that the infanticide occurs to Medea as a direct result of the Aegeus scene, but as Easterling, 'Infanticide', 185 points out, 'Euripides does not make exactly clear when Medea arrives at the details of her plan, and we cannot say that the encounter with Aegeus gave her the idea to kill the children'. Moreover, the importance of children is stressed in Medea's encounters with Creon (cf. 282-3, 329, 344-5) and Jason (558-67, 596-7) as well as with Aegeus.

58. When they hear this, the audience may recall the story that the Corinthians killed Medea's children out of revenge. But Euripides signals his radically different version when Medea says that she will not leave her children in Corinth to be mistreated by her enemies (781-2). I agree with Page, *Medea*, 129, *pace* Diggle, that Brunck's case against 782 is weak.

59. The audience would be aware of a further irony in Medea's promise, for she later tried to kill Aegeus' son Theseus in Athens (cf. above on the *Aegeus* plays).

60. Some think that Medea goes into the house at this point to prepare the poisonous gifts for Jason's new wife, but there is no need for her to do so: the supposed inconsistency (cf. 789, 950-1) is detected only on the page, not in performance. Gredley (n. 38), 33-4, by contrast, thinks that 'her disappearance into the invisible space of the house emblemizes the first steps in her disconnection from humanity'. However, there are good dramatic reasons for placing Medea's significant exit later (see below on 1250). In any case, the last two stanzas of the Chorus' song are much more effective if Medea is present to hear them. A. Lesky, *Greek Tragic Poetry* (New Haven: Yale University Press, 1983), 458 n. 28 suggests that Medea goes into the house during the first strophic pair, then returns to hear the second, but such ingenuity is unnecessary.

61. U. Hübner, 'Zum fünften Epeisodion der *Medea* des Euripides', *Hermes* 112 (1984), 401-18, p. 403 thinks that the children go into the house with the Paidagogos, but the scene is far more effective if they are present with Medea. There is also clear evidence in the text that they remain on stage (e.g. 1040-1).

62. Different editors are prone to delete different parts of Medea's monologue (Diggle's OCT marks the whole of 1056-80 as interpolated), but the speech is dramatically effective as it stands: cf. Chapter 4.

63. On tragic dochmiacs, cf. M.L. West, *Greek Metre* (Oxford: Oxford University Press, 1982), 108, who observes 'Their tone is always urgent or emotional.' Aristophanes occasionally parodies the metre, e.g. *Birds* 1188-95.

64. Segal, 'Vengeance', 170.

65. In contrast to the surviving plays of Aeschylus and Sophocles, children in Euripides occasionally speak or sing, and their words always intensify the scene's emotional register.

66. Segal, 'Vengeance', 174.

67. The chariot is held aloft by the *mêchanê*, a type of crane used to stage flying entrances and exits, usually of divine figures (contrast Aristophanes, *Peace* 79-177, where the mortal Trygaeus, using the crane, flies to heaven on a dung-beetle). As with other such entrances in tragedy, Medea is probably swung into view above the *skênê* and then deposited upon the roof before beginning her speech: cf. *Andromache* 1228-30, *Electra* 1233-7. An ancient commentator on the play says that the chariot was pulled by winged snakes (cf. OCT p. 88, Hypothesis (a) line 9), and Medea appears with such a chariot in a number of fourth-century Italian vases: cf. *LIMC*, 'Medeia', nos. 29, 35-8. It is therefore often argued that a dragon-chariot was used in the original Athenian performance; though far from certain (perhaps the snakes were used in a later South Italian production?), this is an attractive hypothesis, not least because of Medea's long-standing association with snakes, chthonic symbols of poison, magic, and death: cf. *LIMC*, 'Medeia', nos. 3-6, a series of four Attic lekythoi from the last quarter of the sixth century BC showing Medea's head surrounded by snakes.

68. We have already heard Medea's complaints against Jason, especially in their *agôn* and the Aegeus scene.

69. A nearly identical passage of concluding anapaests (but with a different first line) is found at the end of *Alcestis, Andromache, Helen,* and *Bacchae*. Page, *Medea*, 181 remarks: 'There is little doubt that these lines were a floating epilogue which could be attached to the end of any play.' Kovacs (n. 54) 65-7, however, defends *Medea* 1415-19, arguing that Euripides has adapted his own ending to *Alcestis* and inserted an appropriate reference to Zeus as 'steward' (1415; cf. 169-70, where the Nurse describes Medea's invocation of 'Zeus steward of oaths').

2. Husbands and Wives

1. Cf. Knox, 'Medea', 219: 'in the intellectual ferment of late fifth-century Athens, the problem of women's role in society and family was, like everything else, a subject for discussion and reappraisal.' For the Sophists' discussion of women's status and rights, see G.B. Kerferd, *The Sophistic Movement* (Cambridge: Cambridge University Press, 1981), 159-62.

2. Among the thirty-two extant tragedies only Sophocles' *Philoctetes* has no female characters.

3. Cf. Chapter 1, nn. 3-4.

4. Even if it could be proved that women did *not* attend the dramatic competitions at the City Dionysia, this would not rid the plays of their power to interrogate the gender-based division of power and authority in Athenian society.

5. In his production of 438 BC (*Cretan Women, Alcmaeon in Psophis, Telephus, Alcestis*) Euripides substituted *Alcestis* for the satyr-play which regularly followed the three tragedies.

6. E. Hall, 'The Sociology of Athenian Tragedy', in P.E. Easterling (ed.), *The Cambridge Companion*, 93-126, p. 109.

7. F. Zeitlin, 'Playing the Other: Theater, Theatricality, and the Feminine in Greek Drama', in J.J. Winkler and F.I. Zeitlin (eds), *Nothing to Do with Dionysus?* (Princeton: Princeton University Press, 1990), 63-96, pp. 68-9.

8. As C. Pelling, *Literary Texts and the Greek Historian* (London: Routledge, 2000), 200 puts it, individual viewers will have found 'different ways to become absorbed in the play and to pose the moral issue'.

9. Cf. e.g. Thucydides 2.45.2; D. Schaps, 'The Women Least Mentioned: Etiquette and Women's Names', *Classical Quarterly* 27 (1977), 323-30.

10. L. McClure, *Spoken Like a Woman: Speech and Gender in Athenian Drama* (Princeton: Princeton University Press, 1999), 4.

11. For the 'honourable' ideal of women remaining indoors, cf. Xenophon, *Oeconomicus* 7.30. However, it is important to bear in mind that what men say to other men in public (for example, in law-court speeches) about their wives and daughters (for example, that they never go out) does not necessarily reflect what women actually do. Cf. D. Cohen, *Law, Sexuality, and Society: The Enforcement of Morals in Classical Athens* (Cambridge: Cambridge University Press, 1991), 159: 'In such communities [traditional Mediterranean societies] the sexual politics of space and labor are far more complex than the thesis of seclusion and isolation would allow.'

12. J. Gould, 'Law, Custom, and Myth: Aspects of the Social Position of Women in Classical Athens', *Journal of Hellenic Studies* 100 (1980), 38-59, pp. 43-4. [Reprinted in J. Gould, *Myth, Ritual, Memory and Exchange: Essays in Greek Literature and Culture* (Oxford: Oxford University Press, 2001), 112-57.]

13. Along with an elevated status, the citizenship law meant that Athenian women's sexual mores would be guarded even more keenly than before. The obsession with pure Athenian blood presumably encouraged the Athenian myth of autochthony (cf. *Ion* 265-74).

14. C.B. Patterson, 'Hai Attikai: The Other Athenians', *Helios* 13 (1987), 49-67, p. 53.

15. While Athenian democracy can be seen as a system that gives certain rights and privileges to citizen males by excluding such 'outsiders' as women, slaves, and foreigners, this does not mean that democratic forms of government were necessarily any more hostile to women than non-democratic ones. Indeed, Aristotle argues that women have more freedoms under democracy than under aristocracy or oligarchy (*Politics* 1313b33, 1319b28).

16. Easterling, 'Infanticide', 180-1. Contrast the situation of Andromache: like Medea she is supplanted by a young Greek royal wife, but she is continually aware of her inferior status as Neoptolemus' enslaved mistress (cf. *Andromache* 29-31).

17. 'Women in Tragic Space', *Bulletin of the Institute of Classical Studies* 34 (1987), 15-26, p. 24.

18. G. Gellie, 'The Character of Medea', *Bulletin of the Institute of Classical Studies* 35 (1988), 15-22, p. 16.

19. Cf. J. Gould, 'Dramatic Character and "Human Intelligibility" in Greek Tragedy', *Proceedings of the Cambridge Philological Society* 24 (1978), 43-67 [reprinted in Gould (n. 12), 78-111], pp. 52-4, who exaggerates the extent to which Medea's series of lyric outbursts 'prefigures the later "fragmentation" of Medea's dramatic personality' (p. 53), and who calls Medea (p. 52) 'a fragmented, disjoint figure, abstractly seized'.

20. According to Gellie (n. 18), 22, Medea's various characteristics mean that 'it is hard to engage with Medea and therefore with the play'.

21. For Medea's skilful self-presentation as an average fifth-century woman, see E. McDermott, *Euripides' Medea: The Incarnation of Disorder* (University Park: Pennsylvania State University Press, 1989), 43-64.

22. Since the divorcing husband had to return the dowry to the wife's family, 'it was a safeguard for the woman and her relatives against divorce' (D.M. MacDowell, *The Law in Classical Athens* (London: Thames and Hudson, 1978), 88). Plato attacks the dowry from a reactionary male perspective as a source of female power and independence (*Laws* 774c). Not surprisingly, Medea also overlooks the fact that she herself married against her father's wishes and without a dowry.

23. For Medea's 'abduction' from Colchis, cf. Herodotus 1.2.

24. Pelling (n. 8), 205.

25. Girls received only a minimal education; cf. W.K. Lacey, *The Family in Classical Greece* (Ithaca: Cornell University Press, 1968), 163. Moreover, as S. Halliwell, 'Between Public and Private: Tragedy and Athenian Experience of Rhetoric', in C. Pelling (ed.), *Greek Tragedy and the Historian* (Oxford: Oxford University Press, 1997), 121-41, p. 134 points out, 'the dangerous power of [female] rhetoric ... is borrowed from the world of male discourse'.

26. Cf. Easterling (n. 17), 15 '[women's] biological closeness to untamed nature fits them for dark activities like the use of magic, as well as making them disturbingly unpredictable.'

27. Knox, 'Medea', 222.

28. Cf. B. Gredley, 'The Place and Time of Victory: Euripides' *Medea*', *Bulletin of the Institute of Classical Studies* 34 (1987), 27-39, p. 30: '[Creon] tries to salvage something of his authority by a second proclamation which merely formalizes Medea's victory.'

29. For Medea's heroic self-conception, cf. Chapter 4.

30. Gould (n. 12), 57.

31. Cf. *Ion* 1090-8, where a Chorus of Athenian women claim that songs do women no justice and merely mask male faults.

32. Cf. J.M. Snyder, *The Woman and the Lyre: Women Writers in Classical Greece and Rome* (Carbondale: Southern Illinois University Press, 1989), 1-63 on the female poets of Archaic and Classical Greece (none of whom came from Athens).

33. M. Williamson, 'A Woman's Place in Euripides' *Medea*', in A. Powell (ed.), *Euripides, Women and Sexuality* (London: Routledge, 1990), 16-31, p. 28 faults the Chorus for merely saying that women are no worse than men, but this is a radical statement in context.

34. Cf. K.J. Reckford, 'Medea's First Exit', *Transactions of the American Philological Association* 99 (1968), 329-59, p. 334: 'Most obviously in the first scene with Jason, Medea airs her outraged feelings: she is as honest here in helplessness as later, in the exodos, after victory.'

35. By betraying her family and relinquishing her royal status in Colchis, Medea made herself dependent upon Jason; cf. 502-3, 506-8. Yet he has exploited her vulnerability, knowing that she has no *philoi* to protect her.

36. Medea's strong sense of fidelity to Jason is that of an exemplary wife, a quality which makes her eventual infanticide all the more shocking.

37. A. Lesky, *Greek Tragic Poetry* (New Haven: Yale University Press, 1983), 222.

38. R.B. Palmer, 'An Apology for Jason: A Study of Euripides' *Medea*', *Classical Journal* 53 (1957), 49-55, p. 51.

39. Even if, in the heroic world of the play, Medea's standing as Jason's legitimate wife is never questioned; cf. n. 16.

40. Cf. e.g. *Hippolytus* 616-24.

41. Cf. A. Carson, 'Putting Her in Her Place: Women, Dirt, and Desire', in D.M. Halperin, J.J. Winkler, F.I. Zeitlin (eds), *Before Sexuality: The Construction of Erotic Experience in the Ancient Greek World* (Princeton: Princeton University Press, 1990), 135-69, p. 159: 'In sum, the female body, the female psyche, the female social life, and the female moral life are penetrable, porous, mutable, and subject to defilement all the time.' As Gould (n. 12), 55-6 notes, Greek myth features many sexy women who destroy men.

42. Cf. G.O. Hutchinson, *Greek Lyric Poetry* (Oxford: Oxford University Press, 2001), 466 on 659-61: 'The [choral] narrator does here (more generally) what the Nurse had declined to do (83): she curses those like Jason.'

43. One might also contrast Euripides' handling of a similar triangle (one Greek man, two women – one Greek, one foreign) in *Andromache* (c. 425 BC), where Neoptolemus' new Greek wife, Hermione, aims to kill her husband's former concubine, the enslaved Andromache, whose skill with drugs, Hermione claims, has made her infertile.

44. Nevertheless, the fact that it was the norm did not stop Plato from objecting to men playing women on the grounds that it would deprave them both psychologically and morally (cf. *Republic* 395d5-e2).

45. S.A. Barlow, 'Euripides' *Medea*: A Subversive Play?', in A. Griffiths (ed.), *Stage Directions* (London: Institute of Classical Studies, Supplement 66, 1995), 36-45, p. 43.

46. Cf. G.M.A. Grube, *The Drama of Euripides* (London: Methuen, 1941), 163: 'The death of Creon, who would otherwise have rushed to avenge himself on Medea, keeps the tragedy that of Medea and Jason.'

47. Lines 1233-5, in which the Chorus express pity for Creon's daughter, are deleted by many editors as a sentimental interpolation. But it is not impossible that the Chorus should distinguish between Jason's justified ruin and the unmerited death of his new wife.

48. Similarly, although the audience may feel sympathy for Jason's grief, they may also regard him as at fault for only now realising the value of his children (cf. 1399-1402).

49. H. Foley, 'Medea's Divided Self', *Classical Antiquity* 8 (1989), 61-85, p. 83; cf. C. Sourvinou-Inwood, 'Medea at a Shifting Distance', in Clauss and Johnston (eds), *Medea*, 253-96, p. 261, who thinks that Medea 'can generate a certain empathy both for herself and for the position of women in general in a way that does not appear to threaten the central male self of the audience'.

50. N.S. Rabinowitz, *Anxiety Veiled: Euripides and the Traffic in Women* (Ithaca: Cornell University Press, 1993), 150.

3. Greeks and Others

1. Unlike the exclusively Athenian festival of the Lenaea (cf. Aristophanes, *Acharnians* 504-6), the audience at the Dionysia came from all parts of the Greek world: cf. Pickard-Cambridge, *Dramatic Festivals*, 58-9, Csapo and Slater, *The Context of Ancient Drama*, 286-7.

2. Page, *Medea*, xxi.

3. Cf. e.g. E. Hall, *Inventing the Barbarian: Greek Self-Definition through Tragedy* (Oxford: Oxford University Press, 1989), N. Loraux, *The Children of Athena* (Princeton: Princeton University Press, 1993), 184-236, P. Vidal-Naquet, 'The Place and Status of Foreigners in Athenian Tragedy', in C. Pelling (ed.), *Greek Tragedy and the Historian* (Oxford: Oxford University Press, 1997), 109-19.

4. As Jason puts it, a person's reputation among barbarians is irrelevant; only Greek opinion counts (539-41).

5. Herodotus presents the Greek pantheon of twelve gods as having been taken over from Egypt (cf. 2.3.2, 43-5, 49-58). However, even if an awareness of this kind extended to a popular level, one may doubt whether it detracted from the popular feeling that Greeks (and their gods) were naturally superior. Indeed, despite Herodotus' own awareness of other cultures and their different *nomoi* ('customs'), his narrative suggests that he too holds Greek culture and morality to be the best; cf. R. Thomas, *Herodotus in Context: Ethnography, Science and the Art of Persuasion* (Cambridge: Cambridge University Press, 2000), 101 on 'the distinction that runs throughout the *Histories* between Greeks and barbarians'. On religious borrowings, see J. Rudhardt, 'De l'attitude des grecs à l'égard des religions étrangères', *Revue de l'histoire des religions* 209 (1992), 219-38 [translated in T. Harrison (ed.), *Greeks and Barbarians* (Edinburgh: Edinburgh University Press, 2002), 172-85], T. Harrison, *Divinity and History: The Religion of Herodotus* (Oxford: Oxford University Press, 2000), 208-22, 251-64.

6. [Xenophon], *Constitution of the Athenians*, 2.8; cf. also 2.7 on Athens' 'luxurious' international cuisine. Fifth-century Athenians also welcomed foreign gods into their religious life (cf. Plato, *Republic* 327a-328a); Aristophanes is said to have written a comedy in which foreign gods were put on trial and expelled from the city (Cicero, *Laws* 2.37). See R. Parker, *Athenian Religion: A History* (Oxford: Oxford University Press, 1996), 152-98.

7. The creation and maintenance of different ethnic identities within Greece (e.g. between Dorians and Ionians) is discussed by J.M. Hall, *Ethnic Identity in Greek Antiquity* (Cambridge: Cambridge University Press, 1997), who observes (p. 182) 'Ethnic identity is not a "natural" fact of life; it is something that needs to be actively proclaimed, reclaimed and disclaimed through discursive channels. For this reason, it is the literary evidence which must constitute the first and final frame of analysis in the study of ancient ethnicity.' Athenian difference (and superiority to other Greek communities) was supported by the myth of autochthony, the idea that the Athenians were born from the soil of Attica itself; non-autochthonous groups were, by contrast, merely migrants.

8. Cf. Plato, *Laws* 693a, *Republic* 470a-71b. A hardening of the sense of Greek superiority was aided by the fact that in Athens nearly all slaves and many metics (or resident aliens) were by origin non-Greek. Aristotle rationalised the *status quo* by arguing that barbarians were in any case 'naturally' slaves (*Politics* 1252b5-9). Though metics could amass great wealth and occasionally even hold public office (cf. Plato, *Ion* 541c-d), they were not able to own land in Attica and their status was inferior to that of any Athenian citizen; cf. D. Whitehead, *The Ideology of the Athenian Metic* (Cambridge: Cambridge Philological Society, Supplement 4, 1977).

9. Cf. Antiphon fr. 44B.27-35 DK on the essential sameness of barbarian and Greek: 'For we all breathe the air through our mouth and nostrils and eat food with our hands.' Thucydides' Pericles (2.39.1) praises Athens' openness to outsiders (even at her own risk).

10. See A. Diller, *Race Mixture among the Greeks before Alexander* (Westport, Connecticut: Greenwood Press, 1971; orig. publ. 1937), 32-56.

11. The effects of Greek colonisation are complex: on the one hand, contact between settlers and non-Greek locals might lead to hybrid practices or artefacts; on the other hand, cultural interaction between settlers and native communities might (at the same time) lead to an enhanced sense of Greek difference and identity.

12. For references, see Hall (n. 3), 19-55, C. Tuplin, 'Greek Racism? Observations on the Character and Limits of Greek Ethnic Prejudice', in G.R. Tsetskhladze (ed.), *Ancient Greeks West and East* (Leiden: Brill, 1999), 47-75, pp. 54-5.

13. Diller (n. 10), 22.

14. It also led to a new fifth- and fourth-century version of 'Panhellenism' understood specifically as a union of Greek states against Persia: cf. M.A. Flower, 'From Simonides to Isocrates: The Fifth-Century Origins of Fourth-Century Panhellenism', *Classical Antiquity* 19 (2000), 65-101.

15. For the inferior military skills of the Persians, cf. Herodotus 5.49, 7.101-4, 9.62.

16. Tuplin (n. 12) asks whether the Greek view can be considered racist and argues that in Greece (p. 62) 'foreigners are not primarily marginalised because of physical or genetic differences'. However, even if this is true, one may still speak of a battery of assumptions which together express a form of Greek cultural racism. Greekness is memorably defined by Herodotus in terms of common blood, language, religion, and culture (8.144).

17. Popular Greek thought generally opposes the categories of human, male, Greek, and free to those of animal, female, barbarian, and slave: cf. K.J. Dover, *Greek Popular Morality in the Time of Plato and Aristotle* (Oxford: Blackwell, 1974), 74-102, 114-16. For criticism of the denigration of women and barbarians, see *Iphigenia in Aulis* 1394, 1400-1 (in context).

18. According to a scholiast on Pindar, *Olympian* 13.74, Medea saved the Corinthians from famine by sacrificing to Demeter. If this story were well known in Athens (which is not impossible), Euripides may have intended the audience to be reminded of it here. Yet the Nurse's remark may simply be vague rather than allusive (Medea does not mention the famine in her supplication of Creon), so that the audience imagine Medea using her knowledge of drugs and magic to help the Corinthians in various unspecified ways. (Medea raises one of these benefits in her later scene with Aegeus: 716-18).

19. S. Lawrence, 'Audience Uncertainty and Euripides' *Medea*', *Hermes* 125 (1997), 49-55, p. 49, observes of the prologue that 'if the audience entered the theatre expecting to see Medea the exotic criminal, they received essentially ... the opposite impression'.

20. Unable to return home to Colchis (166-7, 502-3), Medea's exile from Corinth leaves her *apolis* ('without a city'; cf. 359-61, 386-9). To be cityless represented an extreme form of degradation in Greek society (cf. 645-6), and it is a status explored in many tragedies (e.g. Sophocles, *Philoctetes*, *Oedipus at Colonus*; Euripides, *Electra*, *Iphigenia in Tauris*, *Orestes*).

21. According to Herodotus, when the Persians offered terms of peace after the battle of Salamis in 480 BC, the Spartans urged the Athenians to reject them 'since you know that there is neither trust nor truth among barbarians' (8.142.5).

22. 'The Earliest Jason: What's in a Name?', *Greece and Rome* 48 (2001), 1-17, p. 14.

23. Cf. 395-7, where the liminal goddess of magic, Hecate, is said to be at the hearth, the symbolic heart of Medea's household.

24. G. Gellie, 'The Character of Medea', *Bulletin of the Institute of Classical Studies* 35 (1988), 15-22, p. 18 asks 'what is to stop us asking silly questions like ... Why did not she and the two boys fly away on the equivalent of a magic carpet to the equivalent of South America?' The answer is 'the play'.

25. Cf. R. Friedrich, 'Medea Apolis: On Euripides' Dramatization of the Crisis of the Polis', in A.H. Sommerstein, S. Halliwell, J. Henderson, B. Zimmermann (eds), *Tragedy, Comedy and the Polis* (Bari: Levante, 1993), 219-39, p. 222: 'In short, Medea is thoroughly Hellenized by being heroized.'

26. C. Gill, *Personality in Greek Epic, Tragedy and Philosophy: The Self in Dialogue* (Oxford: Oxford University Press, 1996), 162.

27. Of course, the Athenian law, if interpreted strictly, would disadvantage the offspring of Jason's new marriage as well, since Jason is not a native Corinthian. Nevertheless, although the connections between the pre-legal world of the play and fifth-century Athens are more oblique, the play does focus on Medea's status as a foreign (non-citizen) wife, and the contemporary Athenian situation helps the audience see why she might be discarded.

28. G.M.A. Grube, *The Drama of Euripides* (London: Methuen, 1941), 157.

29. Some scholars detect a political (anti-Corinthian) subtext here as well (Corinth exiles helpless suppliants, Athens takes them in) and relate this to the tensions between the two cities at the start of the Peloponnesian War; cf. e.g. A.M. Moreau, *Le mythe de Jason et Médée. Le va-nu-pied et la sorcière* (Paris: Les Belles Lettres, 1994), 167-70.

30. See below on 1384-5. The Aegeus scene itself is full of ironies (cf. Chapter 1 on the motif of childlessness). Medea does not 'solve' Apollo's oracle, since Theseus will be born despite it. And so when Medea arrives in Athens, Aegeus does not really need her help, since he already has a son.

31. For the particularly decorative language used here in praise of Athens, see T.B.L. Webster, *The Tragedies of Euripides* (London: Methuen, 1967), 283-4.

32. As D.J. Conacher, *Euripidean Drama: Myth, Theme and Structure* (Toronto: University of Toronto Press, 1967), 193 observes, the Chorus' stress on the clash between polluted infanticide and pure Athens is 'an effective way of expressing the self-destruction which her plans involve'.

33. Cf. C. Pelling, *Literary Texts and the Greek Historian* (London: Routledge, 2000), 180: 'it is to Athens' credit that she can afford such refuge, even if it is going to be abused: compassion is not simply self-interest, and is still valuable even when gratitude turns sour. Reality, not the Athenian ideal, is defective.'

34. Of course, Aegeus has no idea of Medea's infanticide when he makes his promise, but there is more to the situation than autochthonous Athenians (cf. 825-6) plagued by an impious outsider.

35. Cf. *Andromache* 173-6 (the Spartan Hermione accuses the 'barbarian race' of incest and kin murder); Hall (n. 3), 188 'it was one of Euripides' favourite sources of irony to explore the tension between the outrageous acts which were the very stuff of Greek myth and the contemporary ideology which claimed that only barbarians committed such deeds.'

36. Page, *Medea*, xxi.

37. Since vase-paintings dated after 431 BC frequently portray Medea in foreign dress, Page, *Medea*, lxii n. 1 may be right to see Euripides' original production as the source of Medea's 'oriental costume'. In a detailed discussion of the vases (with illustrations), C. Sourvinou-Inwood, 'Medea at a Shifting Distance', in Clauss and Johnston (eds), *Medea*, 253-96, pp. 279-91 has argued that Medea wore *Greek* dress *until* her final appearance in Helios' chariot. On this model, the infanticide marks a crucial turning-point, and (p. 291):

'Now he [Jason] sees her in her true colors: a barbarian.' Yet Jason has already stressed the Greek / barbarian distinction long before the final scene (536-41). Although the notion of (initial) Greek costume is attractive (it would fit in well with Medea's claim that she did her best to adopt Greek ways), the text never mentions Medea's dress and the vase-painting evidence is inconclusive. If Medea did wear foreign costume from the start, the final scene will have drawn attention to it in a strikingly unsettling way by presenting her as simultaneously foreign and superhuman.

38. Cf. R. Rehm, *Marriage to Death: The Conflation of Wedding and Funeral Rituals in Greek Tragedy* (Princeton: Princeton University Press, 1994), 201 n. 46: 'the verb *synoikêsousa* can mean "living in wedlock", so used by Medea at 242.' Medea's marriage to Aegeus is made explicit in the first hypothesis (10-11). Medea's son Medos (or Medeios), eponymous ruler of the Medes (cf. Aeschylus, *Persians* 765, Hellanicus *FGrH* 4 F 132, Herodotus 7.62.1), is said to have been fathered by Jason in our earliest source ([Hes.] *Theog.* 1000-2, a passage probably written in the sixth century BC), but it seems likely that 'in the fifth century some Athenian tragedians were making Medos out to be the son of Medea and Aegeus' (P. Georges, *Barbarian Asia and the Greek Experience* (Baltimore: Johns Hopkins University Press, 1994), 68). Such a son would explain Medea's eagerness to get rid of Theseus, but we cannot be sure that this version of Medos' birth predates Euripides' *Medea* (perhaps it was developed from it?). However, if Sophocles or Euripides had previously handled the myth in this way (making the Athenians and the Medes related!), an awareness of this would greatly add to the play's deconstruction of the Greek / barbarian divide.

39. As argued by A.P. Burnett, 'Connubial Revenge: Euripides' *Medea*', in *Revenge in Attic and Later Tragedy* (Berkeley: University of California Press, 1998), 192-224, p. 224 n. 130; but cf. Chapter 1 above.

40. S. Saïd, 'Grecs et barbares dans les tragédies d'Euripide. La fin des différences?', *Ktema* 9 (1984), 27-53 [translated in Harrison (n. 5), 62-100], p. 27 n. 2, counts 101 examples of *barbaros* in eighteen tragedies (including [*Rhesus*]), as against 14 in the seven extant tragedies of Aeschylus, and six in the seven tragedies of Sophocles. The Greek / barbarian distinction was also prominent in *Philoctetes*, one of *Medea*'s companion plays in 431 BC; cf. C.W. Müller, 'Euripides' *Philoctetes* as a Political Play', in Sommerstein (n. 25), 241-52, pp. 247-8. As Pelling (n. 33), 208 notes, in tragedy such polarities are 'a way of exploring, not a mental straitjacket'.

41. Hall (n. 3), 222, who remarks: 'Euripides' overturning of the orthodoxy in regard to the relative worth of Greek and barbarian is the paradigm of the rule-proving exception.'

42. Tuplin (n. 12), 73 overlooks Euripides when he speaks of 'the absence of any demonstrable intellectually serious challenge to those [ethnocentric] prejudices'.

4. Medea's Revenge

1. I am baffled that J.-W. Beck, *Euripides Medea: Dramatisches Vorbild oder mißlungene Konzeption?* (Göttingen: Vandenhoeck and Ruprecht, 1998), 34-5 can see *Medea*'s allegedly 'poor plot' as the reason for its third place in the dramatic competition.

2. For a detailed discussion of this basic principle of Greek popular thought, see M. W. Blundell, *Helping Friends and Harming Enemies* (Cambridge: Cambridge University Press, 1989), 26-59.

3. For Medea's 'heroic temper', see Knox, 'Medea', 196-9.

4. The Nurse's claim that music cannot heal pain (195-200) suggests that Medea's own mental disharmony will not be easily resolved.

5. For a similar failure to take Medea's grievances seriously, cf. Page, *Medea*, xix, who speaks of her 'childish surprise at falsehoods and broken promises'.

6. A.P. Burnett, 'Connubial Revenge: Euripides' *Medea*', in *Revenge in Attic and Later Tragedy* (Berkeley: University of California Press, 1998), 192-224, p. 205 n. 73 remarks perceptively on Aegeus' appearance: 'In terms of standard revenge structure this is the recognition scene, and it works as such scenes do to consolidate the tactical position of the avenger, while it adds to his [Aegeus'] humanity. Medea is unique, however, in that she does not share either the planning or the prosecution of her intrigue with her ally.'

7. In the winter of 431 BC, just a few months after the production of *Medea*, Pericles is said to have consoled the parents of the Athenian war dead with the thought that 'hope of other sons may strengthen you' (Thucydides 2.44). This is not an option for Jason: his ruin is absolute (cf. 1394-6).

8. As M. Golden, 'Did the Ancients Care when their Children Died?', *Greece and Rome* 35 (1988), 152-63, points out, the high infant mortality rate meant that parents cherished even more those children who survived the difficult early years, especially sons.

9. For killing the children of one's enemy as a form of revenge wherein 'the punishment fits the crime', see J. Mossman, *Wild Justice: A Study of Euripides' Hecuba* (Oxford: Oxford University Press, 1995), 188-9.

10. C. Gill, *Personality in Greek Epic, Tragedy and Philosophy: The Self in Dialogue* (Oxford: Oxford University Press, 1996), 168 well describes the infanticide as an 'exemplary gesture': Medea reasserts the fact that they are '*his children*, and not items to be exchanged for other, projected children or to be included in a scheme for maximizing his happiness'. Jason's selfish view of his children (present and future) is well discussed by D. Ebener, 'Zum Motiv des Kindermordes in der *Medeia*', *Rheinisches Museum* 104 (1961), 213-24.

11. For a detailed review of previous scholarship on the passage, see D. Kovacs, 'On Medea's Great Monologue (Eur. *Medea* 1021-80)', *Classical Quarterly* 36 (1986), 343-52, pp. 343-8, and B. Seidensticker, 'Euripides, *Medea* 1056-80: An Interpolation?', in M. Griffith and D.J. Mastronarde (eds.), *Cabinet of the Muses* (Atlanta: Scholars Press, 1990), 89-102, p. 99 n. 1. U. Hübner, 'Zum fünften Epeisodion der *Medea* des Euripides', *Hermes* 112 (1984), 401-18, p. 415 goes even further and would delete all of 1040-80 on the grounds that Medea thus emerges as a 'unified character' with 'tragic greatness'. But this is to completely misunderstand the force of the speech: on the contrary, as we shall see below, Medea's hesitation enhances the tragic impact of the scene.

12. However, B. Marzullo, 'La "coscienza" di Medea (Eur. *Med.* 1078-80)', *Philologus* 143 (1999), 191-210, p. 191, referring to an unpublished lecture given by Diggle in Delphi in July 1998, reports that Diggle now accepts the authenticity of certain parts of the monologue, and would delete only 1044-8 and 1053-66.

13. Kovacs (n. 11), 348-52, for example, argues that only 1056-64 need be considered suspect, since 1058 and 1059-61 are internally inconsistent, and without 1056-64 (p. 349) 'There is now only one weakening of purpose, that in 1040-7. Thereafter Medea recovers the firmness of her resolve and keeps it, in spite of the wrenching of her maternal feelings, to the very end of the speech.' While it may seem attractive to delete 1056-64, where the no / yes pattern is repeated, the case against them is not overwhelming, given the dramatic and psychological effectiveness of Medea's prolonged and anguished uncertainty. Cf. also Seidensticker (n. 11), 95: 'Kovacs' excision of 1056-64, while removing most of the real and supposed problems of the passage, leaves us with a rather unsatisfactory transition from 1055 to 1065.'

14. Commenting on scholars who delete the whole passage, B. Williams, *Shame and Necessity* (Berkeley: University of California Press, 1993), 205 n. 39 observes 'Their proposals offer a striking example of the pretensions of textual criticism when it is not controlled by a sense of its function.'

15. That they do not go in immediately is made clear by 1069ff., where Medea embraces them. As D.J. Mastronarde, *Contact and Discontinuity: Some Conventions of Speech and Action on the Greek Tragic Stage* (Berkeley: University of California Publications, Classical Studies 21, 1979), 110 points out, the children are stopped by Medea's behaviour and there is no inconsistency here which could be used to support the theory of interpolation.

16. The latent (and seemingly blasphemous) suggestion that the children's death might please the gods is worked out with great force in the final scene of the play.

17. Many scholars have seen here proof of interpolation, but as Page, *Medea*, 149 remarks (on 1058): 'The "inconsistency" with 1059ff. is intensely moving and dramatic: emendation or deletion destroys all the force of Medea's changes of temper.'

18. In the background stands the version of the myth in which the children were killed by the Corinthians to avenge the attack on their royal family (cf. 1238-9). Lines 1062-3 are identical to 1240-1, and the sequence of thought in 1238-41 is the same as that in 1059-63, but this does not prove that either lines are interpolated. It is quite plausible to see Medea repeating the key arguments of her great speech just before her climactic exit to kill her sons inside the house (1250).

19. Cf. G.W. Most, 'Two Problems in the Third Stasimon of Euripides' *Medea*', *Classical Philology* 94 (1999), 20-35, p. 35; also W. Sale, *Existentialism and Euripides: Sickness, Tragedy, and Divinity in the Medea, the Hippolytus, and the Bacchae* (Berwick: Aureal, 1977), 33 on Medea's 'sick' personality: '[She] falsely insists to herself that she is compelled to kill her children, that there is no other way. This insistence we have identified as an avoidance of guilt, a blatant rationalisation.' On the contrary, Medea takes responsibility for the infanticide and never denies its wickedness, while at the same time she regards Jason as the real cause (cf. 1073-4, addressed to the children, 'What you had here your father has taken away'). Her speech represents a desperate internal struggle, not a rationalisation.

20. Cf. Easterling, 'Infanticide', 189 on the dramatic 'master-stroke' of 1059ff. 'She is filled, in fact, with a sudden sense that she is caught in the tide of events and has no longer any choice.'

21. This passage is the central example in ch. 1 of J. Annas, *Ancient Philosophy: A Very Short Introduction* (Oxford: Oxford University Press, 2000), where it is used it to illustrate the different Platonic and Stoic conceptions of the soul.

22. Cf. e.g. A. Lesky, *Greek Tragic Poetry* (New Haven: Yale University Press, 1983), 227, who takes *bouleumata* to refer to the various deliberations of the speech thus far, and who sees Medea's *thumos* as 'stronger than all rational thought'. For Euripides allegedly responding here to the 'Socratic Paradox' (Socrates thought that if one truly knew what was right, one would do it), see T. Irwin, 'Euripides and Socrates', *Classical Philology* 78 (1983), 183-97, p. 197. However, though he is not necessarily replying to Socrates, Euripides is clearly engaging with a basic feature of human behaviour (knowing what is right but not doing it).

23. Cf. e.g. G. Rickert, 'Akrasia and Euripides' *Medea*', *Harvard Studies in Classical Philology* 91 (1987), 91-117, pp. 99-101, H. Foley,

'Medea's Divided Self', *Classical Antiquity* 8 (1989), 61-85, p. 63: 'In my view, this is the Roman dramatist Seneca's Medea, not Euripides.'

24. Gill (n. 10), 217.

25. Cf. H. Lloyd-Jones, 'Euripides, *Medea* 1056-80', *Würzburger Jahrbuch für die Altertumswissenschaft* 6 (1980), 51-9 [= *Greek Epic, Lyric, and Tragedy* (Oxford: Oxford University Press, 1990), ch. 38], p. 58: 'in itself the word *bouleumata* is colourless; it takes its colour from the context. Here the meaning is made clear by Medea's immediately preceding statement that she knows what evil she is about to do.'

26. A. Hobbs, *Plato and the Hero: Courage, Manliness and the Impersonal Good* (Cambridge: Cambridge University Press, 2000), 141 n. 14 well describes the *thumos* as a 'living repository of Homeric values'.

27. When Medea hails the Messenger's deadly report as 'most beautiful' (1127), he is stunned and asks whether she is perhaps mad (1129); the issue of Medea's sanity will be of particular significance in the case of the infanticide (cf. 1284).

28. Though other child-killing mothers appear in Greek myth, the Corinthian Chorus know only of Ino, whose worship as a sea-goddess (under the name Leucothea) was especially strong in Corinth (cf. *Iphigenia in Tauris* 270-1). In a more familiar version of the myth one of Ino's sons was killed by her husband Athamas, who had been driven mad by Hera (cf. *Heracles* and Agave's divinely controlled infanticide in *Bacchae*); Ino then jumped into the sea with her other son and they both drowned. This choral song is the only place where Ino is said to have killed both her sons, making her a closer model for Medea; cf. R.M. Newton, 'Ino in Euripides' *Medea*', *American Journal of Philology* 106 (1985), 496-502, p. 501.

29. In Neophron's *Medea* (cf. Chapter 1), Medea is overcome by a 'bloody madness' (*phoinia lussa*) before killing her sons: Euripides' version is more unsettling.

30. Medea's *deus*-like escape resolves the issue of how she will escape from Corinth (cf. 725-30) in a particularly surprising and provocative manner; cf. I. Worthington, 'The Ending of Euripides' *Medea*', *Hermes* 118 (1990), 502-5.

31. Contrast the guilt-stricken grief of Theseus (*Hippolytus*), Heracles (*Heracles*), and Agave (*Bacchae*). In addition to complicating our sympathy for Medea, the infanticide also affects our view of Jason, who now expresses a pathetic wish to touch his sons (1399-400, 1402-3). However, though his grief is genuine, Medea's retort is compelling: 'Now you speak to them, now you embrace them, though then you thrust them away' (1401-2). Tragically, Jason realises too late what he has lost. Yet the focus throughout the play on Medea's genuine love for her children, and the agony of her decision to kill them, suggest that her grief will be far more intense than his.

32. Cf. D.J. Mastronarde, 'Actors on High: The Skene Roof, the Crane, and the Gods in Attic Drama', *Classical Antiquity* 9 (1990), 247-94, p. 280: 'the demarcation of a separate space, as well as a separate form of locomotion commonly reserved for the gods, creates at times a powerful visual token of the social, ethical, and psychological separation between mortal and divine.' Thus, in escaping as she does, Medea crosses the boundaries which separate the powers of humans from those of the gods.

33. Cf. Hippolytus' impossible wish, 'If only mortals could curse the gods!' (*Hippolytus* 1415). A.N. Michelini, 'Neophron and Euripides' *Medea* 1056-80', *Transactions of the American Philological Association* 119 (1989), 115-35, p. 134 remarks that Medea appears 'by dramaturgical sleight of hand ... like a kind of parody divinity', but this seems to underestimate the seriousness of her transformation.

34. For Medea as a divine figure in early Greek myth, see Chapter 1.

35. According to Medea, Jason will be struck on the head by a part of the *Argo*. Two versions of the myth are known from ancient sources (cf. T. Gantz, *Early Greek Myth: A Guide to Literary and Artistic Sources* (Baltimore: Johns Hopkins University Press, 1993) 371): Jason is killed by a falling timber while sleeping beneath his ship, or he is struck by the *Argo*'s prow (cf. 1335), which he had hung up as a dedication in a temple of Hera. Though both deaths are far from heroic, the latter also implies the hostility of Hera (cf. 1379) and so may be the version recalled here.

36. Cf. S.I. Johnston, 'Corinthian Medea and the Cult of Hera Akraia', in Clauss and Johnston (eds), *Medea*, 44-70, pp. 50-1.

37. In previous versions of the myth, the children were killed either accidentally by Medea or deliberately by the Corinthians (see Chapter 1). As F. Dunn, 'Euripides and the Rites of Hera Akraia', *Greek, Roman and Byzantine Studies* 35 (1994), 103-15, p. 114 observes, Medea's wording at 1380 ('so that none of my enemies may do outrage to them') and 1383 ('in recompense for this unholy murder') evokes the more familiar account, i.e. that of the Corinthians' guilt.

38. Cf. Dunn (n. 37), 114: 'Rather than fashioning a plot that will explain existing customs, he refashions customs in accordance with his plot.'

39. In so doing she refutes Jason's description of her as a 'polluted child-killer' (1346). Also, as S.P. Mills, 'The Sorrows of Medea', *Classical Philology* 75 (1980), 289-96, p. 296 n. 30 observes, by establishing the rites herself Medea 'effectively denies participation in any mourning ritual to Jason; this is the finishing touch to her revenge'.

40. D. Kovacs, 'Zeus in Euripides' *Medea*', *American Journal of Philology* 114 (1993), 45-70, pp. 51-3 collects and discusses the play's many references to the gods, which are neglected by Easterling, 'Infanticide', 177: 'Then there is the striking absence of a cosmic frame of reference: we are given no sense of divine motivation or sanction or control.'

41. Compare, for example, the troubling punishments inflicted by Aphrodite and Artemis (*Hippolytus*), Hera (*Heracles*), Athena (*Trojan Women*), and Dionysus (*Bacchae*).

42. This point is well explored by C. Wildberg, 'Piety as Service, Epiphany as Reciprocity: Two Observations on the Religious Meaning of the Gods in Euripides', *Illinois Classical Studies* 24-5 (1999-2000), 235-56, p. 244.

43. M.P. Cunningham, 'Medea APO MÊCHANÊS', *Classical Philology* 49 (1954), 151-60, p. 153 speaks of Medea's 'loss of her own humanity'. According to R. Friedrich, 'Medea Apolis: On Euripides' Dramatization of the Crisis of the Polis', in A.H. Sommerstein et al. (eds.), *Tragedy, Comedy and the Polis* (Bari: Levante, 1993), 219-39, pp. 230-1 'The exodos shows her, dehumanised by her deed and metamorphosed into a Fury of revenge, as the personification of an irrational elemental force.' For D.J. Conacher, *Euripidean Drama: Myth, Theme and Structure* (Toronto: University of Toronto Press, 1967), 198, the ending expresses 'the transformation of a human heroine back to the folk-tale fiend of magic powers'. Others focus on Medea's loss of 'womanhood' as a result of the infanticide: e.g. L. Galis, 'Medea's Metamorphosis', *Eranos* 90 (1992), 65-81, p. 80, E. Schlesinger, 'On Euripides' *Medea*', in E. Segal (ed.), *Euripides: A Collection of Critical Essays* (Englewood Cliffs: Prentice Hall, 1968), 70-89, p. 89: 'The granddaughter of Helios may stand in triumph on her dragon-chariot, but Medea the woman is dead.'

44. Medea's departure may be god-like, but the bitter stichomythia between her and Jason is still largely that of an estranged husband and wife.

45. Some critics see Medea's revenge as an attack on the 'heroic code' itself; cf. R. Rehm, *Marriage to Death: The Conflation of Wedding and Funeral Rituals in Greek Tragedy* (Princeton: Princeton University Press, 1994), 149: 'the play condemns Medea's murdering her children and, more importantly, exposes the dangers inherent in the principle that leads her to do it.' However, rather than undermining the ethics of revenge *per se*, Medea's decision reveals her tragically straitened capabilities as a woman.

46. See Segal, 'Vengeance', 17.

47. Cf. Gill (n. 10), 173: 'we are encouraged to see the ethical force of her grounds for acting as she does while sharing her repugnance for the act, and the consequences, of infanticide.'

48. S.A. Barlow, 'Stereotype and Reversal in Euripides' *Medea*', *Greece and Rome* 36 (1989), 158-71, p. 170.

49. *Pace* Foley (n. 23), 82, Medea is not transformed into 'an amoral deity'. Segal, 'Vengeance', 22 contrasts the human solidarity at the end of *Hippolytus*, *Heracles*, and *Bacchae* with the absolute alienation here. Despite its harshness, however, the ending of *Medea* is far from being 'nihilistic', as argued by E. McDermott, *Euripides' Medea: The Incarnation of Disorder* (University Park: Pennsylvania State University Press, 1989), 65-79, who claims (p. 8) that Euripides 'ultimately leaves his audience foundationless'. On the contrary, as we have seen in the preceding chapters, the play's questioning of social, political, and ethical norms has a profoundly stimulating and constructive effect.

5. Multi-Medea

1. More generally, though Euripides' plays met with comparatively modest success in the dramatic competitions of fifth-century Athens (see Chapter 1), changes in theatrical taste meant that they enjoyed an unrivalled popularity both in Athens and beyond in the following centuries. For the cultural factors underlying Euripides' posthumous success, see G. Xanthakis-Karamanos, *Studies in Fourth-Century Tragedy* (Athens: Athenian Academy, 1980), B.M.W. Knox, 'Euripides: The Poet as Prophet', in P. Burian (ed.), *Directions in Euripidean Criticism: A Collection of Essays* (Durham: Duke University Press, 1985), 1-12, P.E. Easterling, 'From Repertoire to Canon', in *The Cambridge Companion to Greek Tragedy*, 211-27.

2. For recent studies of this fascinating topic, see the Guide to Further Reading, section 5.

3. A.H. Sommerstein, *Greek Drama and Dramatists* (London: Routledge, 2002), 61.

4. For an extensive study of Medea in both Greek and Roman art, see M. Schmidt, 'Medeia', *LIMC* (1992) 6.1.386-98 (discussion), 6.2.194-202 (illustrations).

5. Nos 35 and 36 in Schmidt's catalogue.

6. Apollonius was probably also influenced by Antimachus' narrative elegy *Lyde* (c. 400 BC), which included the story of Medea and Jason's disastrous love affair.

7. Besides being a poet, Apollonius was in charge of the royal library at Alexandria.

8. R.L. Hunter (ed.), *Apollonius of Rhodes: Argonautica III* (Cambridge: Cambridge University Press, 1989), 19.

9. Cf. the irony of *Argonautica* 3.997-1004, 1096-101, where Jason encourages Medea to support him by appealing to the story of Ariadne's help for Theseus; as the audience know, Theseus later abandoned Ariadne on the island of Naxos.

10. For detailed discussion of these plays, see A. Arcellaschi, *Médée dans le théâtre latin d'Ennius à Sénèque* (Rome: École française de Rome, 1990), 37-195, O. Ribbeck, *Die Römische Tragödie im Zeitalter* *der Republik* (Teubner: Leipzig, 1875), 318-25, 528-36. For Medea's popularity as a subject in Roman art (especially wall-paintings and sarcophagi), see V. Zinserling-Paul, 'Zum Bild der Medea in der antiken Kunst', *Klio* 61 (1979) 407-36, pp. 428-36.

11. Relating Medea's reunion with Medus, her son by Aegeus, in Colchis; for a translation of the fragments, see E.H. Warmington, *Remains of Old Latin*, vol. 2 (Cambridge, Mass.: Harvard University Press, 1936), 248-65.

12. Probably set in Scythia and presenting the murder of Medea's brother Apsyrtus during the escape from Colchis (cf. Warmington (n. 11), 456-65).

13. On the basis of the surviving fragments, some scholars believe that Ennius wrote a second Medea play, set in Athens (and possibly based on Euripides' *Aegeus*); see H.D. Jocelyn, *The Tragedies of Ennius* (Cambridge: Cambridge University Press, 1969), 45, 342-50. Ennius' adaptation of Euripides is therefore more strictly referred to as *Medea exul* ('Medea in Exile') to distinguish it from the other play.

14. That is, whereas Euripides has the Nurse wish that the Argo had never sailed to Colchis, and then wish that the pine had never been cut to build the ship (1-4), Ennius puts her wishes in chronological order.

15. On Augustus' fondness for Greek drama, see C.P. Jones, 'Greek Drama in the Roman Empire', in R. Scodel (ed.), *Theater and Society in the Classical World* (Ann Arbor: Michigan University Press, 1993), 39-52, p. 44.

16. Ovid himself is far from bashful about his skills as a writer of tragedy: cf. *Amores* 2.18.13-14, 3.1, *Tristia* 2.553-4.

17. Cf. Quintilian, *Institutio oratoria* 8.5.6, Seneca, *Suasoriae* 3.7. Given so little text, A.G. Nikolaidis, 'Some Observations on Ovid's Lost *Medea*', *Latomus* 44 (1985), 383-7, seems unfairly critical of the play's literary quality. Though the play has not been preserved, this does not mean that it was bad, and the remarks of Tacitus and Quintilian suggest that it was considered a classic of the Roman stage.

18. For Medea's various roles in Ovid's poetry, see Arcellaschi (n. 10), 231-47, S. Hinds, 'Medea in Ovid: Scenes from the Life of an Intertextual Heroine', *Materiali e Discussioni* 30 (1993), 9-47.

19. *Tristia* 3.9 narrates the murder of Medea's brother at *Tomis*, deriving its name from the Greek verb *temnô* ('I cut'), because Medea cut up her brother's limbs there and scattered them to delay her father's pursuit.

20. Whether Seneca wrote his tragedies for performance, as opposed to recitation or private reading, remains a controversial issue; cf. G.W.M. Harrison (ed.), *Seneca in Performance* (London: Duckworth, 2000).

21. To avert the threat of retribution from Pelias' son Acastus (not found in Euripides), Creon and Jason put the blame for Pelias' murder entirely on Medea (256-65).

22. In Seneca's version, unlike Euripides', Creon's decree of banishment applies only to Medea, not to her children, and she is to go into exile alone.

23. Seneca ignores Horace's advice that 'Medea should not murder her children in view of the audience' (*Ars Poetica* 185).

24. Seneca's play has no Aegeus scene and we are not told where Medea will go after leaving Corinth.

25. Cf. Seneca's far greater emphasis on Medea's magical powers (especially 675-842).

26. As does Easterling, 'Infanticide', 188-9.

27. For the play's relation to (Seneca's) Stoic philosophy, and particularly the Stoic view of the emotions, see H.M. Hine (ed.), *Seneca: Medea* (Warminster: Aris and Phillips, 2000), 2-3, 27-30. At his death in AD 65 the poet Lucan, Seneca's nephew, is said to have left an unfinished tragedy *Medea*, but we know nothing of it. Valerius Flaccus' unfinished epic *Argonautica* exploits Euripides, Apollonius, and Seneca, as 'Medea's grim future is the subject of emphatic and repeated irony in the poem' (G.O. Hutchinson, *Latin Literature from Seneca to Juvenal* (Oxford: Oxford University Press, 1993), 70).

28. The Archive of Performances of Greek and Roman Drama (Oxford) lists over 500 entries for *Medea* between the 1540s and the present day, and new items are continually being added. The great rise in productions of *Medea* in the late twentieth century is in part linked to the tremendous impact of feminism.

29. For the topical resonances of Corneille's 'tragedy of witchcraft and political corruption', see F. Macintosh, 'Introduction: The Performer in Performance', in E. Hall, F. Macintosh, O. Taplin (eds), *Medea in Performance: 1500-2000* (Oxford: Legenda, 2000), 9.

30. *Medeamaterial* (1983) follows Euripides' story of betrayal, but consists largely of a long monologue by Medea. Müller also wrote a pantomime, *Medeaspiel* (1974), which ends with Medea tearing up her child and throwing it at Jason.

31. Medea is played by the renowned opera diva Maria Callas, who had often sung the title-role in Cherubini's *Médée* (composed in 1797).

32. I. Christie, 'Between Magic and Realism: Medea on Film', in Hall, Macintosh, Taplin (n. 29), 144-65, p. 153; cf. D. Mimoso-Ruiz, 'Le mythe de Médée au cinéma', *Pallas* 45 (1996), 251-68.

33. *Medea: Stimmen* (Darmstadt: Luchterhand, 1996). [*Medea: A Modern Retelling* trans. J. Cullen (London: Virago, 1998).]

34. While many modern treatments of the myth follow Euripides in seeking to understand (or justify) Medea's reasons for infanticide (cf. J. Kerrigan, *Revenge Tragedy: Aeschylus to Armageddon* (Oxford:

Oxford University Press, 1996), 315-42), Wolf's Medea is scapegoated as a child-killer because of sexual and racial hostility.

35. K. von Fritz, 'Die Entwicklung der Iason-Medea-Sage und die Medea des Euripides', *Antike und Abendland* 8 (1959), 33-106, p. 47.

Guide to Further Reading

The bibliography to *Medea* is vast. This guide offers a selection (especially brief in §4) of some particularly accessible and stimulating works
on the play and its cultural background. For fuller coverage, and
discussion of specific points, see the items referred to in the notes.

Abbreviations

DK = H. Diels and W. Kranz (eds), *Die Fragmente der Vorsokratiker*
(6th edn, Berlin: Weidmann, 1951-2).

EGF = M. Davies (ed.), *Epicorum Graecorum Fragmenta* (Göttingen:
Vandenhoeck and Ruprecht, 1988).

FGrH = F. Jacoby (ed.), *Die Fragmente der griechischen Historiker*
(Leiden: Brill, 1923-58).

IEG = M.L. West (ed.), *Iambi et Elegi Graeci* (2nd edn, Oxford: Oxford
University Press, 1989-92).

LIMC = H. Ackermann and J.-R. Gisler (eds), *Lexicon Iconographicum
Mythologiae Classicae* (Zurich: Artemis, 1981-97).

PMG = D.L. Page (ed.), *Poetae Melici Graeci* (Oxford: Oxford University Press, 1962).

TrGF I = B. Snell (ed.), *Tragicorum Graecorum Fragmenta*, I (Minor
Poets) revised by R. Kannicht (Göttingen: Vandenhoeck and Ruprecht, 1986).

TrGF IV = S.L. Radt (ed.), *Tragicorum Graecorum Fragmenta*, IV
(Sophocles) (Göttingen: Vandenhoeck and Ruprecht, 1977).

1. Texts and commentaries

J. Diggle, *Euripidis Fabulae* (Oxford: Oxford University Press, 1981-
94). The standard Greek text of Euripides. Three volumes: *Medea*
is in volume one.

A. Elliott (ed.), *Euripides: Medea* (Oxford: Oxford University Press,
1969). Extremely useful and informative edition for beginners;
includes Greek vocabulary.

D.L. Page (ed.), *Euripides: Medea* (Oxford: Oxford University Press, 1938). Still valuable philological commentary, but largely out of date on interpretive issues.

Fortunately, we can look forward to two new editions of *Medea*:

D.J. Mastronarde (ed.), *Euripides: Medea* (Cambridge: Cambridge University Press, 2002).

J. Mossman (ed.), *Euripides: Medea* (Warminster: Aris and Phillips, forthcoming).

2. Translations

R. Blondell, M.-K. Gamel, N.S. Rabinowitz, B. Zweig (eds), *Women on the Edge: Four Plays by Euripides. Alcestis, Medea, Helen, Iphigenia at Aulis* (London: Routledge, 1999).

J. Davie, *Alcestis and Other Plays* (London: Penguin Books, 1996).

D. Kovacs (ed.), *Euripides: Cyclops, Alcestis, Medea* (Cambridge, Mass.: Harvard University Press, 1994).

J. Morwood, *Euripides: Medea and Other Plays* (Oxford: Oxford University Press, 1997).

D.R. Slavitt and S.P. Bovie, *Euripides: Medea, Hecuba, Andromache, Bacchae* (Philadelphia: University of Pennsylvania Press, 1998).

3. Introductions to Greek tragedy

E. Csapo and W.J. Slater (eds), *The Context of Ancient Drama* (Ann Arbor: University of Michigan Press, 1995). Translation of major ancient documents relating to Greek and Roman drama, with detailed commentary and illustrations.

P.E. Easterling (ed.), *The Cambridge Companion to Greek Tragedy* (Cambridge: Cambridge University Press, 1997). A collection of up-to-date essays on all aspects of Greek tragedy, covering its political, religious, and poetic context as well as later reception.

J.R. Green, *Theatre in Ancient Greek Society* (London: Routledge, 1994). A study of Greek drama through the archaeological evidence (vase-painting, terracottas, mosaics, sculpture, etc.).

M. Heath, *The Poetics of Greek Tragedy* (London: Duckworth, 1987). Analysis of the emotional impact and aesthetic enjoyment of the plays.

A.W. Pickard-Cambridge, *The Dramatic Festivals of Athens*. 2nd edn, revised by J. Gould and D.M. Lewis (Oxford: Oxford University Press, 1968). The most comprehensive discussion of the ancient evidence for the Athenian dramatic festivals. Greek is not translated; not for beginners.

O. Taplin, *Greek Tragedy in Action* (London: Routledge, 1978). A study of Greek tragedy in performance, with discussion of nine plays.

4. Books and articles on *Medea*

J.J. Clauss and S.I. Johnston (eds), *Medea: Essays on Medea in Myth, Literature, Philosophy, and Art* (Princeton: Princeton University Press, 1997). A wide-ranging collection of essays; includes extensive bibliography.

P.E. Easterling, 'The Infanticide in Euripides' *Medea*', *Yale Classical Studies* 25 (1977), 177-91. A lucid account of the psychological motives, moral significance, and dramatic impact of Medea's infanticide.

B.M.W. Knox, 'The *Medea* of Euripides', *Yale Classical Studies* 25 (1977), 193-225. Classic study of Medea as a heroic avenger.

C. Segal, 'Euripides' *Medea*: Vengeance, Reversal and Closure', *Pallas* 45 (1996), 15-44. A stimulating discussion of Medea's violent revenge, focussing on her reversal of basic categories of power (male/female, Greek/barbarian, mortal/divine).

5. Studies of *Medea*'s reception in literature, music and art

See also Easterling in section 3 above, Clauss and Johnston in section 4.

B. Gentili and F. Perusino (eds), *Medea nella letteratura e nell'arte* (Venice: Marsilio, 2000).

E. Hall, F. Macintosh and O. Taplin (eds), *Medea in Performance, 1500-2000* (Oxford: Legenda, 2000).

A. Kämmerer, M. Schuchard and A. Speck (eds), *Medeas Wandlungen: Studien zu einem Mythos in Kunst und Wissenschaft* (Heidelberg: Mattes Verlag, 1998).

E. Kepetzis, *Medea in der Bildenden Kunst vom Mittelalter zur Neuzeit* (Frankfurt am Main: Peter Lang, 1997).

D. Mimoso-Ruiz, *Médée antique et moderne* (Paris: Édition Ophrys, 1982).

R. Uglione (ed.), *Atti delle giornate di studio su Medea* (Turin: Celid Editrice, 1997).

Two recent journal issues are also devoted to this topic:

Pallas 45 (1996), *Médée et la violence*.

Der altsprachliche Unterricht 40.4-5 (1997), *Mythen erzählen: Medea*.

Glossary

agôn: contest, argument.

barbaros: non-Greek.

deus / dea ex machina (literally 'god from the machine'): god or goddess who appears on the *mêchanê* to resolve a crisis and reveal the future fate of the main characters.

didaskalos: trainer (of the chorus), producer.

echthros: enemy.

ekkyklêma: trolley which could be rolled out of the central door of the theatre building to display indoor scenes.

mêchanê: crane used for airborne entries and exits (usually of divine figures).

metic: non-Athenian resident of Athens (required to pay a special monthly tax, the *metoikion*).

oikos/oi: household(s).

orchêstra: 'dancing-floor' (sometimes circular), the centre of the performance space.

philia: friendship.

philos/oi: friend(s).

polis/eis: city-state(s).

skênê: theatre building behind the acting area.

stasimon/a: choral song(s).

thumos: heart, spirit, anger.

Chronology

c. 533 BC: Establishment of City Dionysia at Athens

c. 525/4: Birth of Aeschylus

c. 507: Reforms of Cleisthenes; beginning of democracy at Athens

501: City Dionysia reorganised; official contest records begun

c. 499: Aeschylus' first production

c. 496/5: Birth of Sophocles

490: First Persian invasion defeated at Marathon

484: Aeschylus wins dramatic contest for first time

481-479: Second Persian invasion defeated after battles at Artemisium, Thermopylae, Salamis, and Plataea

c. 480: Birth of Euripides

472: Aeschylus' *Persians* wins first prize

468: Sophocles wins first prize in his first dramatic competition

462: Reforms of Ephialtes; extension of democracy at Athens

458: Aeschylus wins first prize with *Oresteia* tetralogy

456/5: Death of Aeschylus

455: Euripides competes for first time and wins third prize (entry includes *Daughters of Pelias*)

451/0: Pericles' citizenship law

449: Competition for best tragic actor begun at City Dionysia

441: Euripides wins dramatic contest for first time (plays unknown)

438: *Alcestis* wins second prize with *Cretan Women, Alcmaeon in Psophis, Telephus*

431: *Medea* wins third prize with *Philoctetes, Dictys, Theristai* (satyr play)

431-404: Peloponnesian War between Athens and Sparta

c. 430-428: *The Children of Heracles*

428: *Hippolytus* (revised version) wins first prize

c. 425: *Andromache*

c. 424: *Hecuba*

c. 424-420: *Suppliant Women*

c. 422-416: *Electra, Heracles*

415: Athenian expedition against Sicily (defeated in 413)

415: *Trojan Women* wins second prize with *Alexander, Palamedes, Sisyphus* (satyr play)

c. 414: *Iphigenia in Tauris*

c. 413: *Ion*

412: *Helen*

c. 412: *Cyclops* (satyr play)

c. 409: *Phoenician Women*

408: *Orestes*

407/6: Death of Euripides in Macedon

406/5: Death of Sophocles

after 406: *Bacchae* and *Iphigenia in Aulis* win first prize posthumously with *Alcmaeon in Corinth*

405: Aristophanes' *Frogs* presents Aeschylus and Euripides competing for the throne of tragedy in the underworld

Index

141